BRINGING OUT THE BEST

A Resource Guide for Parents of Young Gifted Children

by Jacqulyn Saunders
with Pamela Espeland

Free Spirit
PUBLISHING

Library of Congress Cataloging-in-Publication Data

Saunders, Jacqulyn, 1950-
    Bringing out the best.

    Bibliography: p.
    Includes index.
    1. Gifted children — Education (Preschool) — United
States. 2. Parent and child — United States.
I. Espeland, Pamela, 1951-   . II. Title.
LC 3993.218.S38   1986   371.95   86-81129
    ISBN 0-915793-06-7

10 9 8 7 6 5 4 3 2

Printed in the United States of America

Special thanks to students and staff of the International School of Minnesota who appear in the photographs on pages 50, 64, 140, 148, 168, 174 and the front cover of this book. Also thanks to Steve McHugh for the photographs on pages 36, 128 and 184, and Cathy Podezwa for the photographs on pages 4 and 20.

Art Direction: MacLean & Tuminelly
Cover and Text Design: Nancy MacLean
Illustration: Caroline Price
Cover photograph: Steve McHugh
Keyline and art production: Mike Tuminelly

FREE SPIRIT PUBLISHING
123 N. Third St., Suite 716
Minneapolis, MN 55401
(612) 338-2068

CONTENTS

PART III: COPING WITH THE SCHOOLS

PART IV: RESOURCES

Dedication

For Eric and Benjamin, who bring out the best in *everyone*.

J.S.

For my mom, and for my former teachers at the Roy Spalding Elementary School in Glen Ellyn, Illinois. Mrs. Strobel and Mrs. Harms, if you're out there, thanks.

P.L.E.

Acknowledgments

Many people gave generously of their time and expertise while we were working on this book. Special thanks go to computer specialist Sandy Barnes; Linda Silrum of the Twin Cities Metro ECSU Gifted Center; Mary Larson, currently a graduate student in educational psychology and a valuable source of information on parent/child interaction; Mary Apuli, president of the Art Educators of Minnesota; Kathleen Baxter, Coordinator of Children's Services at the Anoka County Library; and Jenny Nelson, copy reader extraordinaire.

We wish to acknowledge Dr. Joseph Renzulli, Dr. Bella Kranz, and Dr. Merle Karnes, noted experts in the development of observational checklists for gifted and talented children, whose work was the inspiration for our checklists in Chapter 1. Thanks to Lorraine Hertz of the Minnesota Department of Education for allowing us to use her chart on I.Q. scores, which also appears in Chapter 1. The work of May V. Seagoe and Sandra Kaplan, along with that of Drs. Renzulli and Kranz, helped us to formulate the admired traits/problem behaviors chart in Chapter 2. The MacPhail Center for the Arts, an extension of the University of Minnesota, provided us with much useful information on choosing music classes for Chapter 5. The Gifted Center of the Educational Cooperative Services Unit/Twin Cities Metro Area in Minnesota wrote the original checklist for choosing a preschool; our adaptation appears in Chapter 8.

Last but most, thanks to Judy G., who brought the two of us together and gave us extra pages when we needed them.

Introduction

The gifted child is a challenge and a joy. Such a child holds special promise but also has special needs that can test the capabilities, endurance, and patience of parents and teachers alike.

This guide is intended to provide parents of gifted children with information regarding the needs of their sons and daughters. It is geared to those with young children, ages two to seven. For the most part, these are parents who are just coming to the realization that their children are gifted and who are exploring the educational and social opportunities available to their children. At this early stage these may be based primarily in the home, or they may be found in the daycare, preschool, or public school setting. This guide describes what parents can do in each of these settings to help ensure that their children will learn according to their abilities and thrive according to their natures.

As you're doubtless already aware, parenting a gifted child is no picnic. Then again, as one mother put it, "It's a nice kind of problem to have." There's something quite wonderful about all that *potential* running about underfoot, badgering you with questions, getting in your hair, and forever reminding you that what you're dealing with is not exactly typical. We've had plenty of contact with gifted children, both personally and professionally, and we know what it's like to alternate between pride and exasperation, wonder at the things coming out of your child's mouth and well-founded fear about the months and years ahead.

It's tempting to get carried away with thoughts of future Nobels, Pulitzers, and presidencies — so tempting, in fact, that we often forget that the complicated creatures who can *seem* so mature with respect to their knowledge, insight, and abilities are just children, and little children at that. It's that thought we have attempted to keep before us in writing this book. Do the same while reading it, and you really will bring out the best in your child.

Jacqulyn Saunders
Pamela Espeland
Minneapolis, 1986

PART I

COMING TO TERMS WITH GIFTEDNESS

CHAPTER 1

How to Tell if Your Child Is Gifted

If you think that your child is gifted in some way (or ways), you're probably right. Research indicates that parents are pretty good at accurately describing the behavior of their children and predicting their later successes in certain fields of endeavor. In fact, when they err, it tends to be on the side of underestimating their children's abilities. This is particularly true if these abilities are paired with a high energy level and a well-developed creative sense.

It's not uncommon for parents to respond with doubt or disbelief on first learning that their child is eligible for gifted programs. ("Are we talking about the same Sid Smith? Short kid, dark hair, always in trouble?") Part of this is because they assume that giftedness has only to do with academic abilities. But children, like the adults they will one day become, can be capable of excellence in several areas, and they don't all have to do with reading, writing, and arithmetic.

The United States government (and many state educational programs) recognizes five general categories in which a child may exhibit special ability. They are:

1. General intellectual ability. This is the child who seems to be just plain smart in a lot of areas. Obvious skills include memorizing facts and developing and applying concepts.

2. Specific academic aptitude. This is the child who focuses by choice on one or two specific areas of endeavor. He or she may be adept at science but inept at or indifferent to writing. The high school math whiz whose hobby is prime factoring license plates may be said to have a specific aptitude.

3. Creative or productive thinking. This is the child who makes you wonder if he or she was born on another planet. When one mother suggested to her gabby three-year-old that they be "quiet as mice" in the car, he responded, "No, let's be quiet as crops." Perhaps you have received similar clues that your child is a creative thinker.

4. Leadership ability. This is the child who can convince almost anyone (not just doting grandparents) to do almost anything. When admiring this ability, it is important to remember that the children who have it won't always lead their peers in directions approved of by teachers and parents.

5. Ability in the visual and/or performing arts. This is the child who loves to dance, sing, draw or paint, play a musical instrument, and/or act. In the early years, high potential in this area may be evidenced as much by passion as by skill. For instance, watch out for the two-year-old who prefers Elvis Presley to nursery rhymes and at age three becomes infatuated with the music of Eric Satie.

Some educators and researchers also recognize a sixth category, and we agree that it should be included:

6. Psychomotor aptitude. This is the child who is expert at manipulating his or her body in time and space. Many children with this gift pass physical milestones early and inspire such cocktail party boasts as "She's only four months old and is already three chapters ahead of herself in the baby book."

"Mom, I don't understand what size has to do with whether or not I can start school."

Do-It-Yourself Assessment Checklists

One of the ways to determine a child's strengths is by comparing his or her behavior with a list of descriptors. A child who exhibits a majority of the characteristics described within a certain category may be identified as having high potential in that area.

The following checklists are most appropriate for children of kindergarten age or younger. A two-year-old with high potential in a certain area would be expected to display *some* of the behaviors described; an older child, *most* of them.

General Intellectual Ability

☐ Asks many specific questions and seriously attends to the answers.

☐ Has a good memory.

☐ Frequently prefers playing with older children.

☐   Has a subtle or mature sense of humor. Is likely to understand puns or plays on words before other children. (Example: Draws cartoons or pictures illustrating figures of speech — "Cat got your tongue?" "*Dead* tired.") May not understand or appreciate the silly or bathroom humor of other children the same age.

☐   Is exceptionally curious. May either use a "scattershot" approach of exploring many areas of interest simultaneously, or focus on one at a time.

☐   Has a high energy level; is restless in mind and body.

☐   Is interested in cause-effect relationships. Likes to explore possible explanations. May insist that his or her explanation makes more sense than the "real" one. (Examples: "Grass grows because worms push it up through the dirt." "The reason people invented airplanes was because their arms got tired and they needed a place to sit down.")

☐   Has a long attention span for activities of own choosing.

☐   Knows many things about which other children the same age are unaware.

☐   Applies concepts of reading and math in contexts other than those in which they were introduced.

☐   Is sensitive to emotional issues at an early age. Asks many questions about pain, death, anger, love, violence, etc.

☐   Is eager to try new activities and/or to perform familiar activities in new ways.

Specific Academic Aptitude

Linguistic aptitude

☐   Uses advanced vocabulary.

☐   Employs advanced sentence structure. (Example: Uses conjunctions like "however" and "although.")

☐   Makes up elaborate stories or fantasies.

☐   Memorizes many poems or stories. Recites poems or rhymes using rhythm and cadence.

☐   Prefers storybooks with many words and fewer pictures.

☐   Has taught (or is teaching) self to read by asking parents or other nearby adults, "What is this letter?" or "What does this word say?" May also learn early by watching TV or by hearing the same books read aloud again and again.

☐ Has an early interest in printing letters, names, and words.

Math/logic aptitude

☐ Is very interested in maps, globes, charts, calendars, and clocks.

☐ Asks many questions about abstract terms, such as time and space. (Example: "When is today *really* tomorrow or yesterday?")

☐ Enjoys assembling new or difficult puzzles.

☐ Likes to count, weigh, measure, or categorize objects.

☐ Recognizes one- and two-digit numbers. Is able to count objects and choose the correct numeral to represent the number. (Example: Counts 11 blocks and points to the numeral 11.)

☐ Understands concepts of money. (Example: Knows that 10 pennies equal a dime.)

Scientific aptitude

☐ Constantly wants to know how and why things work.

☐ Collects things.

☐ Likes to classify and categorize objects and ideas.

☐ Has an advanced understanding of cause-and-effect relationships.

☐ Chooses "how-to" books or nature study books over stories and fairytales.

☐ Likes to take things apart — toys, clocks, flashlights, appliances. May or may not be able to put them back together.

Creative or Productive Thinking

☐ May have an "imaginary friend" and be able to describe him or her in great detail.

☐ Has idiosyncratic speech or mannerisms. May invent words ("thunderclappered") or use graphic and unusual body language. (Example: Gestures dramatically when relating an incident or telling a story.)

☐   Is constantly asking questions.

☐   Responds to questions with a list of possible answers.

☐   Sees solutions that rarely occur to other children or to adults.

☐   Effectively uses materials in ways other than those for which they were intended. (Example: Invents a new game around lotto cards.)

☐   Has a spontaneous sense of humor.

☐   Embellishes stories, TV programs, games, etc.

☐   Makes up elaborate excuses for behavior; finds "loopholes." (Example: "I'm sorry I bit Ralph. But I didn't mean to bite his skin. I only meant to chew his clothes.")

Leadership Ability

☐   Interacts easily with both children and adults.

☐   Is often sought out by other children for play.

☐   Is able to enter an already-playing group of children and be easily accepted.

☐   Offers play suggestions to other children and has them readily accepted.

☐   Is able to influence other children toward his or her own goals, positive or negative.

☐   Understands cause-and-effect as it relates to behavior and consequences. Recognizes when his or her behavior yields certain predictable results.

☐   Has a sense of justice and fair play for both self and others.

Ability in the Visual and/or Performing Arts

Visual arts aptitude

☐   Spends free time drawing, painting, or sculpting.

☐   Remembers in detail items, places, or pictures seen.

☐   Has advanced eye/hand coordination.

□   Embellishes artwork with fine detail.

□   Shows attention to texture, color, and balance.

□   Responds emotionally to photos, paintings, or sculptures, sometimes even those done in abstract or nonrepresentational styles.

□   Shares own feelings and moods through drawings, paintings, or sculptures.

□   Has advanced technical skill in drawing.

Musical aptitude

□   Frequently requests music-related activities.

□   Responds emotionally to music, even in the absence of lyrics. (Example: "That song makes me feel sad.")

□   Can identify a familiar song from the tune only.

□   Sings in tune or close to in tune.

□   Is able to pick out the sound of a particular instrument in a different context from the one in which it was introduced.

□   Prefers poems with lots of sound and rhythm over narrative stories.

□   Dances, moves, or claps in time with musical patterns and rhythms.

□   Is able to sing on the same pitch as a given example. (Samples must be within a child's normal range.)

Psychomotor Aptitude

□   Enjoys movement such as running, jumping, climbing, and/or tumbling as an end in itself.

□   Uses gestures, body movement, and/or facial expression to show or mimic feelings.

□   Has an accurate and relaxed sense of balance when hopping on one foot, walking a narrow line, hanging from a bar, etc.

□   Uses simple athletic equipment with comparative ease. Can accurately throw and catch a softball, jump rope, dribble a basketball, skate, etc.

□   Is able to adapt motor skills appropriately in game situations.

☐ Can hold his or her own in sport-related games with older children.

☐ Creates dances which are vigorous in nature and include much diving, rolling, dipping, and jumping.

Testing

In addition to judging your child's abilities for yourself, you may also choose to have him or her tested by professionals. *Just remember that even the best test can reveal only how a particular child performed particular tasks on a particular day.* In other words, while testing can certainly be informative, it should never be taken as the final word about a child's ability to be successful in any other setting.

Would you want your future to be decided by a group of powerful people who knew nothing about you except your score on a 200-item test you took a month ago? Of course not, and neither would your child.

Standardized testing caught on in a big way around the turn of the century. Today there are as many tests as there are schools of psychology, and their applications are equally diverse. The two types described below are those that parents request most often.

Achievement Tests

Achievement tests measure two things: what a child knows by way of content, and what academic processes he or she can perform. In other words, they do not attempt to measure what a child *can* learn, but what he or she actually *has* learned to date. They do not measure logic, problem-solving abilities, or characteristics of creativity.

Achievement tests will be most useful to you if your child is being asked to spend a large part of the school day going over material you feel he or she has already mastered. In the past, this was not a concern in preschool and kindergarten because children were allowed a wide latitude of choices; recently, however,

many of these settings have become quite standardized and academic in nature. If your child already knows the information and processes being taught, it may be necessary to supplement or enrich the curriculum — or, in the case of a private preschool, to look for an alternative program. Achievement test scores can help you make this kind of decision.

I.Q. Tests

I.Q. tests — also known as ability tests — attempt to measure a child's learning behaviors and ability to learn. I.Q. stands for "Intelligence Quotient." Scores are based on a norm of 100; those who score lower than 90 are considered below average, while those who score over 109 are considered above average.

The following classifications are generally accepted as a working model:

I.Q. Score	Classification	Approximate Incidence in Population
160	Very superior	1 out of 10,000
155	Very superior	3 out of 10,000
150	Very superior	9 out of 10,000
145	Very superior	4 out of 1,000
140	Very superior	7 out of 1,000
135	Superior	2 out of 100
130	Superior	3 out of 100
125	Superior	6 out of 100
120	Superior	11 out of 100
115	Bright	18 out of 100
110	Bright	27 out of 100

Like achievement tests, I.Q. tests may yield valuable information, but in most instances they are given far more emphasis than they deserve. It's been said that you may forget your anniversary or your mother's birthday, but once you know your child's I.Q. score it is burned on your brain forever.

There are several reasons why I.Q. scores should be viewed with some skepticism. For one, many of the most commonly used testing devices are open to charges of cultural bias and may not reflect the potential of minority children. For another, any child from any background is prone to behaviors that will yield significantly lower scores than his or her true ability warrants. Nervousness, separation anxiety, trying too hard to please, or feeling under the weather may result in a child testing poorly. The younger the child, the more likely that one or more of these factors will come into play.

If the child being tested is very bright and creative, there is even more cause to keep the scores in perspective. Consider five-year-old Cindy. When her mother asked how the testing went, Cindy replied, "Fine, but that lady was peculiar."

"What was peculiar about her?" her mother wanted to know.

"Well, she asked such silly questions," Cindy said. "First she asked me what a shoe is. *Everyone* knows what a shoe is! I wouldn't answer. Then she wanted to know the difference between bread and meat. Did she want to know that one used to be a plant and one used to be an animal, or that one is in the protein group and one is in the grain group, or that one is brown and one is white? I didn't know what she wanted, so I wouldn't answer that one either."

Obviously no single factor should be used to determine a child's ability. Instead, assessment should be based on a multidimensional approach. Test scores should be examined in light of parent observation and, if available, teacher observation as well.

Despite the ongoing controversy surrounding I.Q. scores, they do tend to become a part of life for families of children with exceptional general intellectual ability or a number of academic aptitudes. If you're considering I.Q. testing for your child, it helps to know ahead of time what you (and your child) can expect.

Some forms of I.Q. tests are designed to be administered to groups of children, while others are meant to be given individually. It is generally acknowledged that scores from group testing are significantly less accurate. For young children especially, one-on-one testing is the only way to go.

Ideally, your child and the tester — usually a psychologist or psychometrist — will be the only two people in the room while the test is being given. Should your child refuse to be separated from you, you may be allowed to stay, probably seated in such a way that your child will be aware of your presence but unable to see you directly. It is difficult to achieve accurate results with parents around because children are adept at picking up cues from their loved ones, even when these are subconsciously delivered, and they can skew the scores.

The final report should contain a reference to the examiner's assessment of your child's emotional state at the time of testing. It should also list any distractions — your presence, for example, or a fire drill. A typical report might begin like this:

"At four years seven months John is a blue-eyed, left-handed boy with a ready smile. He seemed somewhat hesitant to separate from his mother at first, but appeared to attend comfortably to task once she was gone. He seemed eager to respond to the test items, but did show some fatigue toward the end of the session. I consider the following to be an accurate assessment of his ability."

If, on the other hand, the child exhibited any undue stress or tension, or the parent became involved even inadvertently, the final report would make note of these factors and end with an opinion that the results might *not* be an accurate assessment of the child's ability.

Share with the examiner privately anything you think may affect the scores. One mother called the psychologist the day after her son was tested and said, "I don't mean to be a pushy parent, but is it possible that Fred's scores might have been affected by the fact that his eardrum ruptured a couple of hours later? His pediatrician says that he probably couldn't hear you, and he was experiencing a fair amount of pain at the time." Since Fred was a stoic child who suffered from chronic ear infections, the psychologist might never have known about these developments had the mother not risked being a "pushy parent."

There are many different types of I.Q. tests in use today. Although each measures slightly different abilities, all are designed to assess certain cognitive skills. Your child may be asked to name body parts, describe behaviors appropriate to particular circumstances, and/or use blocks or multicolored pieces of foam or rubber to replicate figures shown by the examiner. There may be items related to arithmetic mastery and math concepts, and items related to vocabulary recognition and use.

Some tests include pictures with pieces missing, and the child is asked to identify the missing parts. Others feature pictures with so many parts missing that they resemble abstract paintings of particular items, and the child is asked to identify the items. Young children may be asked to sequence a series of pictures or to repeat series of numbers backwards and forwards.

Now that you know all this, you may be tempted to make up a few "sample" questions for your child to try. This won't do any harm, but neither will it do any good. Because the items on each test are carefully structured and specifically scored, they cannot be accurately replicated from general descriptions.

Another common parental impulse — and one which *can* do real harm — is to try to help a child "cram" for an I.Q. test. This is a sign of the parent's failure to separate the child's eventual score from his or her own ego. The child senses the parent's anxiety and may be intellectually hamstrung by the fear of "failing" and disappointing the parent. It's a no-win situation all around.

Under the right circumstances — child relaxed, parent absent, no pressure to perform — a test session can be a positive and even enjoyable experience. The child has the opportunity to try out his or her intellectual prowess on some new and diverting problems, and the parent gains one more bit of insight regarding the child's abilities.

□ ■ □

Given this brief introduction to testing, the question remains: Should *you* have *your* child tested? Only you can answer that, because only you know what you will do with the information the testing yields. Ask yourself, "How might we as parents change what we're doing once we have this information?" If the answer is "not much," then you're probably considering testing to satisfy your own curiosity. The question then becomes, "Is it worth it?" Testing requires a large investment of money, time, and energy. While the money may be yours, the time and energy are your child's.

The best reason to test is if you have specific concerns about the educational opportunities available to your child in a specific preschool or elementary school setting. Even though standardized tests are far from perfect, they are still accepted by most institutions as "evidence" of a child's achievements and abilities, and it can be useful to have your child's scores in hand when you go into a conference with school personnel.

Another good reason to test is if you and your family are having a hard time with a child you believe may be gifted. While giftedness is obviously not *the* cause for all behavior problems in children, it certainly can be *one* cause. A child who is physically and emotionally age three but mentally age seven may well be at odds with himself or herself and the world.

Consider four-year-old Karen, who was making her parents crazy by stashing food around the house. They tried everything they knew to get her to stop, but Karen persisted. This strange behavior, coupled with Karen's frequent tantrums and bouts of tears, worried her parents enough that they took her to a psychologist, who administered a battery of personality, ability, and achievement tests.

The tests revealed that Karen's intellectual abilities were in the top one half of one percent of the nation. Knowing this, the psychologist could start asking questions aimed at determining her reasons for hiding food.

It seems that Karen watched the evening news and had a fairly sophisticated awareness of world affairs. She knew that the Middle East was unstable, that terrorists could strike anytime and anywhere, and that millions of refugees were starving. To this adult set of perceptions she applied a solution in keeping with the emotions of a preschooler: Not wanting to be caught with her donuts down, she was stockpiling food in the face of imminent disaster.

Before finding a solution to Karen's problem, it was necessary to understand the motives underlying her behavior. Before doing this, it was necessary to know about her extraordinary ability to process information.

What if you choose to have your child tested and the results just don't "feel right"? The examiner will probably go over them with you in some detail. Ask about those you don't understand, as well as those that surprise or concern you. Find out about the test or tests your child took. Use questions like the following to generate discussion with the examiner:

- Which test was used? What is the examiner's experience with that test? Why was it chosen over others?
- How does the test address the concerns of cultural bias?
- What is the ceiling on the test? (If, for example, a test has a ceiling of 150, it cannot accurately measure an I.Q. above 150.)
- For what type of child was the test originally designed?
- Were your child's scores prorated? (Some examiners will discount very high or very low scores on certain selected items when figuring the final score.)

You should also ask the examiner to describe some of the items on the test and talk about your child's responses to those items.

If you're still not satisfied with the results or the explanations, get a second opinion. Although it's generally not recommended that a child be given an I.Q. test more than once every two to three years, you can certainly take the original scores to another professional for evaluation.

A few final words about testing: Recent work in the field of intelligence assessment may be bringing us back full circle to the kinds of observations and categories used in the checklists. The concept of intelligence is gradually being broadened to encompass other areas than general intellectual ability and specific academic achievement.

For example, in his book, *Frames of Mind: The Theory of Multiple Intelligences* (New York: Basic Books, Inc., 1983), Howard Gardner postulates seven intelligences which are found in most people but differ in terms of how they develop and how quickly they develop. Within this framework a person may be considered to have learning difficulties, to be typical, or to be gifted.

To qualify as an intelligence, according to Gardner, a group of abilities must entail a set of skills which enable an individual to *find, create,* and *solve* problems. If the abilities can be used in this problem-solving manner, they are then examined according to eight characteristics drawn from psychology and sociology. Those abilities which meet most of the criteria are deemed "intelligences."

Gardner claims that intelligences fall into three categories: *object-related, object-free,* and *personal.* Object-related intelligences are those which require an individual to manipulate objects in some physical or symbolic way. They include spatial intelligence, logical-mathematical intelligence, and bodily-kinesthetic intelligence. Object-free intelligences include the free-standing music and language intelligences. Personal intelligences include knowledge of the self (intrapersonal intelligence) and knowledge of others (interpersonal intelligence).

Another proponent of multiple intelligences is Robert Sternberg. In his book, *Beyond I.Q.: A Triarchic Theory of Human Intelligence* (New Rochelle, New York: Cambridge University Press, 1984), he defines three types of intelligence: *contextual, experiential,* and *internal.* An individual uses contextual intelligence to adapt to an environment, change that environment, or choose a different environment better suited to his or her needs. Experiential intelligence builds on past experiences to solve new problems. Internal intelligence is used to approach a problem, evaluate the feedback, and determine whether to change one's approach.

What Gardner, Sternberg, and others are finding is that a person's I.Q. may be a relatively insignificant and even inaccurate measure of what he or she is truly capable of achieving. Future research promises to yield even more interesting theories, some of which may arrive in time to benefit your child.

CHAPTER 2

What It Means to Be Gifted

We all wish for our children that they be bright, happy, and well-adjusted, and most of us consider it our responsibility to make sure they turn out that way. That's why it can be disconcerting to observe in our children abilities that may later set them apart from their peers.

It's natural to have mixed emotions about a child's giftedness. On the one hand, having a youngster who reads at age three or is musically precocious is something to be proud and pleased about. On the other, most of us worry about too much of a good thing. Is it really possible to be *very* bright, happy, and well-adjusted?

Yes, it is. Many gifted children — including those who are sometimes referred to as "severely gifted" — grow up to be autonomous, productive, contented adults. Occasionally this even happens to children who receive *no* support for their special abilities.

For the most part, however, being bright is not in itself a ticket to success. Gifted individuals can be successful, but there is a certain amount of pain and suffering that comes along with the package. To be a child of promise is to be interesting, creative, and exciting. It is also to be at risk for certain emotional problems.

Consider, for example, the traits listed as admired in the following chart. While these characteristics are usually considered positive, carrying them too far can cause problems for a child.

Admired Traits	Problem Behaviors
Verbal proficiency	Talks too much; talks above the heads of his or her age peers
Long attention span	Tunnel vision; resistance to interruption
Rapid learning	Inaccuracy; sloppiness
Creativity	Escape into fantasy; rejection of the norm
Independent learning	Inability to accept help; nonconformity for its own sake
Critical thinking	Critical attitude toward others; perfectionism/ unreasonable standards for self
Preference for complexity	Resistance to simple solutions; overextension of energies

To determine that certain children have special abilities is not to judge them but to describe them. Gifted preschoolers are not any better or worse than other children; they are simply different in some ways, and these differences can become debilitating in later years. Certain social and emotional problems are common to older gifted children, and unfortunately there is no way to predict which might plague your child. What you *can* do is to "inoculate" your child against them with some basic proactive strategies. While these can't guarantee that your son or daughter will sail through youth and adolescence unscathed, they may make growing up a little bit easier.

Strategies for Helping Your Child Belong

High-ability children know that they are different. Many, perhaps most, of the problems they experience stem from this awareness, regardless of whether they can articulate it.

Four-year-olds typically want to be like their parents. Those who have been adopted by families of another race often express a desire to change their skin color, hair texture, or eye shape during this period in order to look more like the parents they love. By age seven they are moving out of the family circle and need to find other children like themselves. For a child whose ability places him or her in the one-in-one hundred range, the possibilities of

finding a real peer are *one in two hundred*. Add the fact that
children this age tend to prefer same-sex playmates and the odds
get even longer.

Whether you are four, seven, forty, or seventy, it is affirming
and comforting to find others who value the same things you do.
Abraham Maslow calls this "the need to belong." It is one of a
hierarchy of needs that he perceives as necessary to becoming a
self-reliant, satisfied, functioning person.

According to Maslow, the basic human needs — for food,
shelter, and safety — are at the bottom level of this hierarchy.
Only after these have been met can an individual move on to the
next level, that of belonging. Here the identity of the self is closely
tied to the identity of the group.

Once that sense of self-as-part-of-a-group has been achieved,
the individual can progress to the next level: turning inward and
developing a sense of self that is independent from the group.
From there he or she can become involved in loving relationships
that involve reciprocal feelings — self-actualization.

What this all adds up to is that ubiquitous term in the childrearing and self-help literature: *self-esteem*. As a parent, you can
help your child to develop a sense of belonging and, by extension,
self-esteem. One way to do this is by devising group situations in
which he or she stands a good chance of being successful.

For very young children, these situations should occur most
often within the family. Whether the family has two members or
ten, each person must be made to feel like an integral part of the
whole. What came "naturally" for past generations may now
have to be more carefully structured. Parents today spend so
much of their time working outside the home, and children spend
so much of theirs in daycare, schools, and recreation programs,
that families must make a deliberate effort to develop a group
identity. Family games, reading sessions, and outings help to satisfy the need to belong and prepare the way for further emotional
growth.

This is especially important for young gifted children because
the next stage of belongingness — fitting into a group *outside* the
family — can be hard for them. It's a painful paradox that the
sophisticated thought patterns that allow such children to under-

stand matters beyond their years are the same ones that keep them from comprehending the simpler behaviors of their peers.

Consider six-year-old Jesse, who made a series of devastating mistakes while on a field trip with her class. On the way, the back seat of the car was filled with first-grade variety bathroom humor. When one wag caused another to inadvertently say "underwear," everyone but Jesse responded with peals of laughter. She remained quiet, even stony-faced. Many miles later, long after the jokes had ended and the children were involved in other activities, she suddenly burst into the conversation with an extremely graphic and somewhat obscene comment. While the other children stared in shocked silence, Jesse went off into peals of maniacal giggling. She later compounded her problem by flinging open a restroom door and exposing to everyone a flustered child perched on the toilet with her Rainbow Brite panties around her ankles.

Through it all, Jesse never understood what went wrong. She loved puns — jokes the other children didn't get. Because she had a sophisticated sense of humor, saying "underwear" or "pee" simply wasn't funny to her. Yet she wanted to belong. So she applied logic to the situation, decided that bathrooms and the invasion of privacy were what the others found amusing, and made a genuine effort to be part of the group. She came away from the experience a near pariah with no idea why.

Jesse's teacher later took her aside and talked about how she was different from the other children. That was certainly a wise and appropriate response, but it was not enough. Jesse needed to be steered toward one or more children with similar abilities and interests. Once she belonged *somewhere*, she might not be so desperate to belong *anywhere*.

Parents should look for one or two settings where appropriate friendships seem likely to develop. Some suggestions:

• **Science, art, or music classes.** Look for those where older and younger children mingle easily and freely.

• **Hobby clubs.** Computer groups or robot clubs can provide common ground even for young children.

• **Any other group that welcomes a meeting of the minds.** This doesn't have to be highly structured. In fact, it's better for young children if it isn't.

If you can't find any of the above in your area, contact your state parent association or educational organization and request any information or advice they might be able to offer (see Part IV, pages 213-221). Or consider starting a group of your own. Or find out if your area music school or art institute has a network of involved families. Or place a notice in your local newspaper stating that you'd like to share certain kinds of activities with a couple of other children and their families.

In other words — take action!

Naturally you won't always be able to create ideal group settings for your child. What about those times when he or she wants to fit into a particular group and just doesn't have any luck? Here are a number of strategies for addressing this problem, some effective and some less so.

•   **The "go-on, get-in-there" approach.** Picture a playground or preschool. A lone child stands to one side of a group of playing children. Behind the child is an adult urging, "Go on, get in there, ask them if you can play!"

While common (what parent hasn't tried it?), this approach is almost always doomed. "May I join you?" works at cocktail parties, but not in sandboxes. Systematic observations of young children in social settings indicate that the popular preschoolers are doers more than talkers. They initiate activity by jumping right in and use short, pointed phrases to give the other children "clues" about what they plan or want to do. Forcing a child to ask, "Can I play?" puts the child in the position of being a supplicant.

•   **Coaching.** This technique was used successfully by a very experienced daycare mom when Peter, a particularly gifted and verbal four-year-old, joined her daycare group. He wasn't interested in many of the activities that the other children were involved in, and he lacked play skills, yet he was clearly worried and hurt because the other kids were enjoying themselves and he was "outside."

The daycare mom started by encouraging Peter to share with her all the wonderful thoughts he was having, and affirming for him the value of the things he chose to do. At the same time, she watched closely for those free-play occasions when he seemed to want to be part of the group. When such an occasion arose, she would take Peter aside and ask, "What are they playing over there?... You're right, it looks like house to me, too. I see a mommy and a daddy and a cat.... Who else might be in that family?" Then the two of them together would prepare a "pretend" role for Peter to try, right down to the details of what he might do and say when he joined the group.

On one occasion Peter decided to be the "baby." He marched into the doll area, sat on the floor, and alternated pretend tears with pronouncements of, "I'm your baby, feed me!" Even though he spent much of that play period being told to sit in a corner, drink his bottle, and "go to sleep now, baby," he seemed satisfied just to be part of the group.

On another occasion he chose to be the plumber. When he arrived on the scene with a real wrench (a stroke of genius on the part of the daycare mom), everyone else decided to be "fixit" types, too, and Peter was the life of the party.

• **Parallel play.** Parallel play — where two children play near each other without interacting much — is a common form of socialization for two- and three-year-olds. By age four most children are starting to respond more directly to playmates and can focus on a shared play theme. However, observations of playgroups indicate that in certain situations preschoolers will revert to parallel play as a way to become assimilated into a group.

A lone child who is unsuccessful in entering an already-formed group may begin playing his or her own version of whatever the group is up to, near enough to be noticed but without crossing the group's "borders." If what the child is doing looks interesting, others may wander over.

There are a couple of keys to making this strategy successful. Because neither comes naturally to many gifted children, you might want to try some light coaching here as well.

• *Make sure that the child is engaged in an activity that the others find appealing.* Novel is good; bizarre is counterproductive. A child who circles the group, flapping his arms and muttering about "playing pterodactyl," is not going to have a positive social experience.

• *Make sure that the child is prepared to welcome the other children.* Many an adult has carefully arranged for a loner to be surrounded by an audience eager to get involved, only to have that child grab every toy within reach and shout, "MINE!" Using toy figures to act out appropriate behaviors in advance can prepare a child for sharing when the time comes.

Countering the Perfectionist Syndrome

Social situations are not the only potholes on the road to self-esteem. Many high-ability children confuse their ability with their self-worth and define themselves in terms of their accomplishments. They become perfectionists — prisoners of their own success for whom nothing but the best is good enough.

They live in fear of making a mistake. Often they are unable to distinguish between times when it's appropriate to give their all and times when it's a waste of emotional energy. Although this is a facet of personality more than ability, it is closely linked to the latter. Successful individuals — those whom society often labels gifted — are certainly driven to succeed. But while drive can be a positive force, too much can lead to perfectionism, which in turn can lead to stress-related physical and emotional problems.

The causes of excessive drive and perfectionism are popular topics in the nature/nurture controversy. It does appear that some individuals are more prone to this behavior than others.

Consider Christopher and Brent, who were born seven months apart to couples who are close friends. Each has turned out to have exceptional thinking and reasoning abilities, and each could be categorized as high-potential. But they approach life very differently — a fact their parents have ample opportunity to notice and comment on, since the two boys spend a lot of time together.

Even before Brent was born, the obstetrical staff at the clinic commented on how active and forceful he was *in utero*. He came into the world determined to conquer it. Unlike the babies in TV commercials who coo their way through bathtime, Brent fiercely waved his limbs, grimly determined to repeat his first accidental splash. Long before his muscles were ready, he wanted to walk, and he would beg to be put into his nylon mesh playpen so he could haul himself up to a standing position. Time and again he would slide down, until he had literally worn a raw spot on the end of his nose from dragging it across the mesh. It was not a pretty sight, and certainly not what his parents had anticipated when they dreamed of their firstborn's first steps.

Christopher, in contrast, was Mr. Mellow. Although he, too, had a need to succeed, he seemed better able to pace himself. His pre-walking days were busy with exploration, but he also spent time carefully observing the locomotion of others. He was in no particular hurry to walk by himself, and when he did get around to it (pretty much on schedule) he required very little practice before he was gracefully strolling about.

The two sets of parents have found it necessary to develop vastly different parenting strategies. Like most new parents, they have been exchanging tips of the trade, and some techniques have been useful in both families. Now that the boys are four, however, their styles are so disparate that all the parents can do at this point is trade anecdotes — some amusing, some bittersweet.

Christopher seems to be less at risk for perfectionism than Brent. When introducing a new situation or task, his parents do it gradually, giving him ample time to consider the possibilities and adapt accordingly. With enough preparation, Christopher is usually satisfied with his performance and himself.

Brent, on the other hand, continues to either throw himself into new situations or refuse to participate, period. Preparation has no effect on him, and, in fact, he resists it, preferring to go it alone. He wants very badly to be good at everything he does, and consequently he sets high standards for himself. In some cases this pays off; in others it doesn't.

For example, his favorite winter activities are skiing and skating, and he is competent at both considering his age. He falls frequently, but that isn't a problem as long as he can get up and start moving again without delay. Swimming is a different story altogether. Brent isn't in control in the pool and must rely on someone else to teach him the proper techniques. Try as he might, he can't yet paddle about on his own, so he has decided that he'd rather not swim at all.

Brent's parents are already trying to help him put success and failure into perspective. One technique that seems to be working is that of modeling the graceful acceptance of one's own mistakes. (Since mistakes come naturally to most parents, this takes almost no advance planning!) Brent often hears his Mom or Dad say, "Well, that didn't go the way I wanted it to. But that's okay." Whenever the family prepares to enter a new situation, the parents talk about things that might go wrong and ways they might respond.

Parents of perfectionism-prone children should also be careful not to overdo it in the praise department. Because praise seems to be such a universally positive thing, parents sometimes forget that it can elicit both healthy and unhealthy responses. With gifted children who do many things early and well, it is easy to fall into a pattern of praise that will aggravate perfectionist tendencies.

"What a good splash, Joey."   "Honey, come look at this."   "Do you think we overdid the encouragement?"

It's perfectly acceptable to reward accomplishment — as long as we don't go too far. Children who are continually praised come to believe that what they can do is more valuable than who they are. And if what you do makes your parents love you, then you'd better be sure that everything you do is worthy of their love.

Consider five-year-old Gina, who refused to bring her violin to school. Her mother simply couldn't understand it. Gina had been taking violin lessons for over a year and played very well. Why was she so sticky on this particular issue?

During a parent-teacher conference, Gina's teacher listened to her mother describe the family theory of home education as a supplement to school. "We encourage Gina to do her older brother's worksheets," Mom explained. "Whenever she gets stuck, we say, 'Keep going; I know you can do it.' Then we praise her when she's successful."

"How do you praise her?" the teacher wanted to know. "Oh, the usual," Mom replied. "We say things like, 'See, I knew you could do it. What a wonderful, bright girl you are. You can do anything you want if you try hard enough.'"

The teacher saw Gina as hesitant to take even the slightest risk (hence her resistance to bringing her violin to school). But when she brought this up in the conference, Mom failed to make the connection between her own extravagant praise and her daughter's fear of failure.

Parents must praise their children's *efforts* as well as their successes. Handling failure appropriately also merits congratulations. For example: "I see that your plaster dinosaur foot fell apart. I like the way you set it aside and moved on to reading your book. Later we can talk about whether you want to try again." In this type of situation, it should be made clear that *whatever* the child decides to do is all right. Choosing to try again will be a lesson in perseverance; choosing to toss the dinosaur foot in the trash will be a lesson in living with one's limitations.

Praise should be given, too, for things that have *nothing to do with ability*. Refraining from hitting one's sister even when she deserves it, sharing a balloon with a friend who popped his, playing with the dog when he needs exercise — all are acts worthy of praise. When care is given to reward these kinds of behaviors as well as more glaring accomplishments, high-ability children will come to define themselves by reasonable internal standards.

Perfectionists also have problems with being too competitive. Even very young students have been known to get disproportionately upset over losing a spelling bee or earning less than a 100 percent score on a quiz.

First-graders Erin and Henry were frequently reduced to tears over their scores on timed math-facts tests. Each family knew that its own child was a wreck, but neither was aware of the other family, nor that the real problem lay in the fact that the two were fairly evenly matched; Erin would "win" one week, and Henry would "win" the next. All the parents knew was that the night before a test was always anxiety-ridden.

The two well-meaning dads each took time to help their young-sters study. They assumed that the more their children knew, the more confident they would be and the less anxious they would feel. Of course, this strategy had precisely the opposite effect. By drilling their kids on the math facts, both fathers were implying that the purpose of the test was to do better and better — which was precisely what Erin and Henry assumed. And because the fathers didn't usually get involved in homework, their doing so on this occasion imbued it with even greater importance.

During the spring conferences, when the teacher discovered what was going on, she encouraged each family to work on relax-ation strategies rather than math facts. By May, Erin and Henry were still apprehensive on test days, but the tears and trips to the school nurse had tapered off.

Interestingly — and significantly — many perfectionist chil-dren have at least one perfectionist parent. Their parents may share other characteristics, like setting unrealistic goals or being too critical. They may do too much for their children, implying that their children can't do anything right. They may be unable to enjoy their own achievements.

Perfectionist parents of perfectionist children need to learn to relax their expectations. They need to give themselves permission to be average at times, and to extend this privilege to their chil-dren. Bright children often need to be guided toward gaining con-trol over their intensity. The following technique, developed in a program for gifted children, can easily be adapted for home use.

Draw up two "certificates" — the more elaborately designed and official-looking, the better. One should read like this:

I, _____, give myself permission to try very hard and be very good at _____.

Signed   Witness

_____   _____

The other should read like this:

```
I, _____, give myself permission to be

NOT so great at_____.


Signed                    Witness


_____    _____
```

Make up a new set of certificates whenever your child seems to need them. And keep a supply on hand for yourself.

Teaching Delayed Gratification

A final problem seen in high-ability children, especially older ones who have been labeled "underachievers," is the inability to delay gratification. Although studies of underachieving youngsters are not yet conclusive, logic tells us that certain contributing behaviors take root early, perhaps in the toddler and preschool years.

Very bright children get accustomed to success. So many things come easily for them that it's tempting to ignore or avoid those that don't. In later years, when other children have a history of struggles to fall back on, some gifted kids find themselves experiencing their first real test of stamina, and they don't feel up to it. Faced with challenging school work or the need to master a body of material or a skill, they prefer not to try. They have no knowledge of what it's like to doggedly persist at something.

One way to sidestep this scenario is by teaching delayed gratification as soon as possible. When a task seems too large for your preschooler, help break it down into steps. Then note whenever each step is accomplished. Or structure some activities at which your child is always successful in such a way that they become a bit tougher. If your child is a whiz at puzzles, for example, find new ones that are slightly more demanding.

Your goal should be to *challenge*, not to frustrate, so be sure to intervene if and when your child shows signs of fatigue or discouragement. For example: "You seem to be having trouble finishing the sailboat. Why not take a break before you get so angry you want to quit? Join me for some milk and a cracker." Over your snack, ask your child when he or she hopes to finish the puzzle. If the goal is unrealistic ("never" or "right away"), help him or her to separate it into smaller pieces. "Why don't you try to get the sail finished today, to show Mom (or Dad) after work? Tomorrow you can choose another part to do."

Children should be encouraged to plan ahead and stick to their plans. The younger the child, the smaller the plan, and the shorter the wait before putting it into operation. For instance, a three-year-old can be given several choices as to what to do after naptime. Upon awakening, he or she should be strongly encouraged to follow through on the original choice. "You said you wanted a banana for a snack, so here's your banana.... You want an apple instead? Well, that would be okay, but do you remember that you chose a banana earlier?"

As children grow older, their choices can extend from bedtime to morning, from day to day, and from weekday to weekend. Ultimately this learning process will stand them in good stead when they must plan a school project and stick to it.

□ ■ □

Specific techniques like those discussed above can help to minimize some of the problems high-ability youngsters face. Virtually *any* technique that develops self-esteem will serve this purpose. Whenever children realize that they are making a valuable contribution just by being themselves, they move one step closer to coping on their own.

One of our favorite games is "I-love-you-because." You can play it anywhere, but it's especially useful on long drives or in waiting rooms.

Start by saying to your child, "Do you know why I love you? I love you because _____." Fill in the blank with anything appropriate. Then the child gets a turn, and it's back to Mom or Dad. Reasons for loving should cover a wide spectrum — from having freckles, to taking baths, to being good at numbers or reading. They can even be silly: "I love you because the sky is blue" is child-sized humor, but it also implies that your child is worth loving just because he or she is part of the scheme of things, like the sky.

The game ends when you say, "I love you because you are _____." Fill in this blank with your child's name.

CHAPTER 3

The (Mixed) Blessing of Parenting a Gifted Child

The gifted child is a child of extremes — in talents and abilities, mood shifts, demands, and delights. The four-year-old who insists on listening only to Duke Ellington can get on your nerves. The three-year-old who refuses to answer to any name but "Ford Factory" can be tiresome. And the toddler who's far advanced in psychomotor abilities can be a trial.

Consider Treesha, who could climb out of her crib and walk long before any of her age peers — and long before she understood half of what her frazzled parents said to her. Every night after Mom and Dad put her to bed, Treesha scaled the walls of her crib, crawled backwards down the stairs, and searched the house until she found her parents. Then she came toward them with a big, proud, nearly toothless grin.

"Go back to bed," her mother would say. "Mommy! Mommy!" Treesha would respond. "To bed," her father would say. "Daddy! Daddy!" tiny Treesha would answer. One of them would haul her back up — and in five minutes Treesha would have made her way back down. Only after she collapsed in exhaustion at her parents' feet (usually sometime around midnight) would Mom or Dad be able to tuck her covers around her for good.

The first few times it happened, Treesha's parents bragged to their friends about how precocious their daughter was. Weeks later, Dad was heard to moan, "*Nobody* wants a child like that."

Then there's Alex, whose ability to think on his feet got him into trouble the first week of first grade. He had long wanted a magnifying glass of his own, and when he saw one on the science shelf he appropriated it and hid it in his desk. His teacher found it and said, "I think this should go back on the shelf, don't you?" Alex replied, "Oh, no, it's mine. I brought it from home." His teacher decided on the direct approach: "Alex, I know you didn't bring it from home. Would you like me to call your Mom and ask her if you have a magnifying glass?" "Go ahead," Alex said, non-plussed. "She doesn't know about every single toy I have." "I don't think that's true," the teacher countered. "Most moms have a pretty good sense of what their kids do and don't have." "I have an idea," said Alex, brightening. "Why don't I donate it to the school?"

Alex's teacher, who was obviously amused by this story, passed it on to the boy's mother. But Alex's mom was not at all amused. To her, this was just the latest in a long line of worrisome behaviors her son had been exhibiting.

Like most books on parenting gifted kids, this one focuses primarily on what you can do to meet the needs of your child. But our experience has taught us that there's far more to it than that. Yes, it's wonderful to have bright children; yes, it's exciting to imagine what they might become — and to see what they already are. It's not all a bed of roses, however. Parenting children of promise takes a toll.

What about *your* needs? Are there ways in which your parenting experiences differ from those of other parents? If so, what can you expect in the coming weeks, months, and years? And what kinds of strategies are available to you *now* for taking care of yourself as well as your child?

We talked to hundreds of parents about their lives with their high-potential children, and many reported parallel experiences and needs. Most agreed that parenting *any* child has certain basic components, regardless of the child's characteristics. All healthy parents love their children, want their children to love them, derive satisfaction from their achievements, fret about their futures, and take great joy in simply being with them. The lives of any parent and child are inextricably bound together, and the child's ability makes no difference in the depth or strength of that attachment.

However, parents of exceptional children also reported that they often feel "different" from the rest of the parent population.

They see their children as presenting unusual and specific challenges that affect how they function in their role as parents — and how they perceive themselves as individuals.

Almost all of the parents we spoke with expressed similar concerns. In the hope that these will be useful to you — if only because they will prove that you're not alone — we present some of them here, along with some possible responses.

I THINK my child may be gifted, but I'm not sure.

As noted earlier, parents are usually right when it comes to assessing their children's abilities. Nevertheless, almost all parents struggle with this issue. They worry that they are not competent to judge, that their opinions are colored by affection for and pride in their children, and that if they settle on an opinion it may be the "wrong" one and result in their doing irreparable damage to their child — either by ignoring talent that should be nurtured, or by pushing for achievement of which the child is not capable.

Parents who wait to make up their minds until their children are older and "formally identified" in school often describe a two-part reaction to the news. The first part goes like this: "Great! I'm so excited and proud; my child is capable of wonderful things!" The second part — which follows closely on the heels of the first — goes like this: "Oh my gosh, what are we going to do now?"

Parents of young children may not have the luxury of outside confirmation of their suspicions, so they may vacillate from day to day, experiencing and re-experiencing those emotions. One day it's, "Is he gifted, or isn't he?" The next day it's, "Look at what he just did. He must be gifted. Isn't that terrific?" Then comes, "Look at what he just did. He must be gifted. This is awful. I can't cope with a kid who's smarter than I am." And then, a week later, "Look at what he just did. He can't possibly be gifted and pull a dumb stunt like that. And besides, Don's daughter is a year younger and reads better than he does.... He's definitely NOT gifted." And that's settled — for the moment.

Granted, most parents don't engage in such monologues, but most *do* have these kinds of thoughts on a semiregular basis. The result is that the issue never comes to closure, and you begin to doubt your own perceptions and your ability to draw sound conclusions from them.

Response: Relax — the label isn't all that important. Your child is who he or she is, and how you feel about it won't make much difference. one way or the other.

DO examine your focus, however. Are you concerned that you have a *gifted* child, or a gifted *child*? Concentrating on the latter can help you regain your perspective.

I feel like I'm being presumptuous to even care whether my child is gifted.

Ours is a supposedly egalitarian society, and to acknowledge that our children have extra ability smacks of elitism. We almost feel guilty admitting that it crosses our minds.

As one mother told a group of parents of gifted preschoolers, "We had Kyle tested when he was three, and the psychologist said his ability is extraordinary — in the one-out-of-one-hundred-thousand range. In the two years since then, I've been attending these group sessions, and I can still hardly get the word 'gifted' out of my mouth. I practically gag on it. Who am I to have a gifted kid?"

Response: Most parents of gifted kids feel this way on occasion. But the more we learn about the special needs of our children, the clearer it becomes that we must acknowledge their abilities if we are going to help them with the special problems they may experience.

On the other hand, an occasional dose of parental modesty is healthy. It helps to remember that not everyone shares our knowledge of or interest in the needs of gifted children, and that there are inappropriate as well as appropriate forums for bringing up the subject.

It *is* presumptuous to refer routinely to "my gifted child." It is *not* presumptuous to know in your heart that your child has special abilities, and to be on the alert for related opportunities and problems.

Remember that the term "gifted" is not a value judgment, but a descriptor. So long as you don't flaunt it, it's no more elitist to describe your child as gifted than it is to describe him or her as freckled or able to ride a bike.

Sometimes I feel intimidated by my own child.

It isn't easy on the ego to have a child who knows more than you do about certain subjects. And it's uncomfortable to realize that there may be times when you can't keep up with a six-year- old. None of us wants our child to look at us with disappointment when we have to answer "I don't know" to questions about electricity, bathroom plumbing, and the nature of God — for the thirty-seventh time in one day.

Not only is this hard on your self-esteem, but it also dents your perceptions of yourself as a parent. As the mother of four-year-old Rachel tells it, "We were at the cabin just when the spring wildflowers were blooming. I had noticed Rachel looking at the wildflower guide during the winter, so I brought it along on our first hike of the season. I had this plan in mind to be Supermom and teach her how to use the guide and look up flowers as we went along. Then we got to the first one, and as I was pulling the book out of my backpack, she said, 'Look, Mom, a columbine! By fall that could be three feet tall!' The rest of the walk went just like that. I love it — and I hate it."

Response: What you may lack in brainpower you'll make up for in experience. Besides, your child got his or her ability from somewhere — your family gene pool, or your home environment, or a combination of the two. Take some credit for both.

It's not always necessary for you to know more than your child, or even to be smarter than he or she is. It *is* important to show more in the way of wisdom, at least during the first couple of decades, and that should be relatively easy. Wisdom takes years to accumulate, and years are what you'll always have more of than your child.

Sometimes I'm frightened for my child.

All parents are anxious about their children's futures, but parents of high-potential children have additional fears unique to their situation. Each of us has heard the horror stories about lonely geniuses, bright adolescents who have gone too far with Dungeons and Dragons, and egghead kids who have resorted to alcohol or drugs to combat their feelings of being different. Add to this the fact that the literature describes gifted children as ultra-sensitive, and parents naturally worry about what will happen to a child who is obsessed at age three with where people go when they die.

Response: Most parents of older gifted children admit that while it was a struggle, their kids appear to be turning out okay. Over and over, they emphasize how important it is to learn as much as possible about your child's special nature. The more you know, the better you'll be able to cope.

Focus on your child's strengths rather than on potential weaknesses. Naturally you'll still worry on occasion, but a realistic assessment of the picture will convince you that the horror stories aren't representative of most gifted kids' behavior. Some studies even indicate that high-ability children have a better than average chance of becoming autonomous, well-adjusted adults.

Keep in mind the concept of the self-fulfilling prophecy. Expect your child to struggle through to adulthood in a relatively happy fashion, and that's probably how things will turn out. This sounds simplistic, but there's a lot of truth to it. How do *you* perform when others around you expect you to fail?

I feel overwhelmed by the responsibility of raising a gifted child.

Many parents report that they were pretty comfortable with their parenting skills — until someone diagnosed their child as gifted. Suddenly being a good parent wasn't good enough.

The mother of five-year-old Larry says, "I've never been very self-confident, but I've really enjoyed being a parent. Larry was an easy baby, and we had a lot of fun together before he started school. Now he's in the gifted program and suddenly my in-laws don't think I can handle a gifted child 'right.' They're always second-guessing us as parents.... Lately it seems like all we do is run to this special lesson and that enriched activity in order to help Larry 'reach his potential.' I need a rest, and I wonder if he doesn't, too."

Response: Children are children first and gifted second. They're happiest when their parents relate to them in a way that makes everyone feel comfortable. How can they be at ease when their parents are always on edge?

Trust your instincts. It also helps to remember that successful individuals are those who have learned to pace themselves. Safeguard your own emotional health by taking parenting one step at a time. (Coincidentally, this is precisely the sort of behavior you want to model for your child.)

When it comes to a child of special ability, there's more at risk from *over*-reacting than from under-reacting. Do what *you* feel right about. And politely, but firmly, let others know that *you're* the parent, thank you very much.

There are times when I feel so isolated.

Parents of gifted kids report that some of their most difficult moments come in conversations with parents of so-called "typical" children. While everyone else rattles on about what their kids are doing, the parents of high-ability youngsters hesitate to describe their children's activities for fear that others will think they are bragging. They also find that other parents are less than sympathetic toward the problems they have with school personnel, or with finding the kinds of resources they need. ("What do you mean, problems? Your kid is getting straight A's. I wish I were so lucky!")

Some parents of promising children have been accused of exaggerating when they talk about their youngsters. Or they've been labeled "pushy" and "too ambitious" for their kids. These are frustrating experiences, and they can leave you feeling alone and lacking in support.

Response: The best way to stop feeling isolated is by joining a group of parents with similar concerns. (For a list of parent organizations, see Part IV, pages 213-217.)

One mother described her reasons for linking up with a state organization for parents of gifted kids: "I don't feel bad talking about my daughter at those meetings. There seems to be a sort of unwritten rule: 'You talk about your kid, I listen, then you owe me and have to listen to one of *my* anecdotes.'"

In addition to putting you together with other parents, these organizations can provide you with information about other resources in your area. They can also advocate (with legislatures and school boards, for example) on behalf of appropriate education for your child and all gifted children.

The more involved you become, the more supportive you will find your group to be. It's a natural outlet for shared experiences, shared concerns, and tales that nobody else would believe.

How to Avoid Parent Burnout

Every parent experiences occasional periods of "parent burnout," and most recover spontaneously after a good night's sleep. But it's possible with *any* special needs child to become overly absorbed in the issues at hand. When this happens, there's a tendency to lose your zest for the job.

Mental health professionals recommend several strategies for avoiding burnout. Here are a few you may find useful as the parent of an especially demanding child:

• **Set realistic goals.** If you have been feeling short on patience lately, try coming up with alternatives to the way you usually respond. Instead of telling yourself, "I will try to answer *every* question Bernie asks," try, "I will answer as many questions as I can. After that, I will help him dial the phone and he can ask Grandma." Rather than deciding, "I will keep up with *everything* Zoe is studying in school," pick one or two subjects you already know or are interested in learning more about.

• **Take breaks from each other.** Once a day, or once a week, set aside a period of time when neither you nor your child must be productive or answer to the other for his or her behavior. If you choose to spend your hour reading a murder mystery at the beach, so be it. If junior and the sitter spend that time mindlessly banging two sticks together in the sandbox, fine.

• **Look for humor wherever you can find it.** Studies have shown that healthy families laugh a lot. Before you lose your cool, think, "What would Bill Cosby do about this?" (Remember: The only reason he and his wife have five children is because they didn't want six.)

• **Start a new activity, or resume one you've neglected in recent years.** You may need to make a few tradeoffs here. Just be sure to order your priorities. Is it worth it to let your child watch a half-hour of marginally appropriate television so you can have time to embroider? Which would do you the most good, sleep or a late-night aerobics class?

• **Maintain your friendships with other adults.** Many new parents find that the time they used to spend with their friends has diminished or disappeared. Although children can keep you busy around the clock, it pays to either maintain relationships with old friends or build new ones with other parents. Then, when you need a favor or a sympathetic ear, your support system will be there for you.

"Who was the counselor your brother was talking about?"

• **Ask for help when you need it.** Because parents of special children bear special burdens, you may experience periods when it all seems like too much to handle on your own. Don't hesitate to seek professional help if you think you need it. As one mother of a difficult six-year-old said, "We suddenly felt that Beth's problems were beyond us. We didn't know what to do next, and although our friends were very supportive we felt we needed more. For us, family therapy was the answer. We had to get over our reluctance — you know, the 'keep-family-problems-in-the-family' attitude most of us grow up with — but it was worth it to get some expert advice."

If you suspect that your child is headed for trouble, it's better to get professional help *now* than to wait until he or she is a teen-ager and out of control.

☐ ■ ☐

Finally: Never forget that parenting a high-potential child has nu-merous rewards. Take pride in watching your child push his or her abilities to their limits. Feel the exhilaration of keeping up with a quick young mind as it leaps from one idea to the next. Let your child show you fresh and unusual ways to perceive the world — something at which gifted children excel. And be prepared for years of surprises; they've only just begun.

PART II

GIFTED PARENTING
AT HOME

CHAPTER 4

You Can Affect
Your Child's Brain
Development

Your child's brain, like your own, contains from 10-15 billion cells. It is shaped like a walnut and colored pinkish-gray. In its lumped and loopy folds is the basis for all that your child is and will become. The quality of the interactions between that three-pound organ and its environment determines the child of today and the adult of tomorrow.

To really understand your special child, you need at least a fundamental understanding of how the brain functions. Our purpose is to tell you just enough to communicate how important your role as parent is in affecting your child's brain development.

The Recommended Reading section at the end of the chapter points the way toward more in-depth and detailed sources of information.

The brain is made of cells called *neurons*. At certain stages of prenatal development, up to a quarter million neurons are grown each minute. At around the time of birth, the number of neurons available to an individual during his or her lifetime becomes fixed. Each of us starts life with only so many brain cells, and we can never add to this number.

It hardly seems fair, then, that these cells may die at rates of up to 10,000 per day from birth onward. They may be lost as a result of alcohol or drug use, illness or injury, or even natural attrition. Luckily, it is estimated that we use only 5-10 percent of the cells available to us, so we can stand to lose quite a few before it starts to matter.

In any event, both the quality and quantity of thought and feeling a particular individual has depends less on the number of neurons than on the type and number of connections which occur between them. It's true that persons who have experienced major damage to one or more portions of their brains usually have more difficulty functioning than those whose brains are intact, but there is still ample evidence that how you use what you've got is as important as what you've got.

And this, of course, is what makes parenting so exciting. Our children enter the world with certain built-in abilities and characteristics, and it is our duty and privilege to help them make the best use of their original equipment. Simply because a child can do something doesn't mean that he or she *will* do it, or should. For a particular child to grow up to compose a sonata, write a poem, develop a theory, or build a family, it is necessary that the neural cells bearing those inherent capabilities make the right connections with other cells.

Each neuron is comprised of three basic parts: the *cell body*, the *axon*, and the *dendrites*. Neurons signal one another through chemical and electrical charges which leave the axons of one and are received by the dendrites of another. A thought or action occurs when these signals jump from neuron to neuron throughout the brain, a process which can generate up to 12 watts of electrical power.

Recent research has indicated that individuals who seem to be especially bright or talented have a superior dendritic structure — in other words, more dendrites in certain cells. In addition, the myelination of the axons — the insulating coating that helps to determine the strength of the impulse a particular cell can send — is greater in those individuals than in persons of "typical" intelligence or ability. It is believed that a cell with more dendrites and a better-insulated axon is able to send more powerful signals and receive more efficiently the signals sent by other cells. It appears that the brain works best when these optimal conditions exist.

That's where we as parents come in. Although the number of neurons a child has is determined at birth, the number of dendrites and the quality of the axon shield has been seen to be affected by environment. This in turn implies that an enriched environment — especially in the early years, when the brain is most plastic — will actually cause the neurons to grow more dendrites and the myelination around the axons to improve. An impoverished environment, in contrast, can cause the existing cells to deteriorate.

A fascinating conclusion may be drawn from all of this. Namely: If the quality of the cells that do the thinking is not fixed, then neither is intelligence.

It's a mistake to believe that parents can "make" a child a genius by properly stimulating his or her brain. Then again, it seems likely that we can provide a setting that encourages whatever they have to flourish. Bright children are often described as having "high potential," and it's important to remember that the word "potential" refers not so much to what they are as to what they might one day be.

Regardless of the original quality of a child's brain cells, the quality of brain material he or she ultimately has can be helped or hurt by the amount of exercise it gets. As the foremost educators of our children, it is both exhilarating and awesome to realize that we have the ability to alter the structure of their brains.

If that isn't enough to keep you awake nights, there are a few more things you should know about the brains in your family. As you may have guessed, brain cells do not just communicate with one another randomly. Instead, they function according to highly complicated and prescribed patterns.

To better understand these patterns, let's look at two popular models of brain function: the *triune brain model,* and the *hemispheric specialization model.*

The Triune Brain Model

Dr. Paul MacLean, Chief of the Laboratory of Brain Evolution and Behavior at the National Institute of Mental Health, has spent the past 30 years developing a theory which divides the brain into three parts: the *reptilian brain,* the *limbic system,* and the *neocortex.*

The reptilian brain is located just above the brainstem and is responsible for such functions as basic survival, self-defense urges, and certain autonomic biological functions.

The limbic system (also known as the "emotional mind") is located at midbrain. Its functions encourage or inhibit memory. Anxiety, anger, sentiment, pleasure, joy, and personal identity are all based in the limbic system. Infant monkeys deprived of certain kinds of stimulation normally provided by mother monkeys show incomplete or damaged dendritic growth in the limbic area, and they grow up to be socially inept and violent.*

The neocortex is the third and largest area of the brain; in essence, it surrounds the other two. Sensory data is processed here, and unlike the reptilian brain and the limbic system, the neocortex has the capacity for verbal communication. It handles logic, analytical thinking, reading, writing, and mathematical processes.

---

* James W. Prescott, "Alienation of Affection," *Psychology Today* (December 1979), p. 124.

While this is a vastly oversimplified description of MacLean's model, it provides us with one basis for understanding why children do not automatically move confidently and enthusiastically from one learning and developmental stage to the next. Problems can and do occur when the three areas of the brain have conflicting needs that prevent them from acting in accord. School teachers have long maintained that children cannot learn when they are hungry, tired, or upset, and these observations are being borne out in brain research. It seems that the parts of the brain can override one another, starting with the reptilian brain.

When a child is hot or cold or hungry or tired, the reptilian brain sends out signals which cause certain parts of the limbic system and large parts of the neocortex to operate at less than full throttle. Apparently the brain's resources are first devoted to comfort and survival, and only when these are assured can it move on to more "sophisticated" thinking.

When a child is angry or frustrated, the limbic system takes over and releases specific transmitters into the neocortex which inhibit cortical function. The "fight-or-flight" impulse takes precedence over logical thinking and problem-solving. What this tells us as parents and educators of our children is that learning best takes place when youngsters are relaxed and comfortable and feel safe. But even this doesn't guarantee success, since the owner of a particular brain is the one who gets to decide whether it's stressed or receptive to new information. A child who is anxious or fearful cannot learn, and it doesn't matter if the fear is unfounded in adult eyes; to the child, it's real. That's why telling a child, "You shouldn't let that bother you," is totally ineffective for dealing with stress.

The parents of three-year-old Ben learned this the hard way. Ben was experiencing recurring night terrors over his belief that the light in his room would turn into a scary TV character. All efforts on his parents' part to solve this problem with logic proved useless. While Ben seemed interested and amused as his mother daily showed him how the TV could be turned on and off, plugged and unplugged ("Look, Ben, we can control it; the character isn't real"), by 2 a.m. he was screaming. And he kept screaming despite his parents' patient middle-of-the-night explanations of reality vs. illusion.

With every passing day, the family became more exhausted and cranky. Finally, one night, Dad flew out of bed and into Ben's room. He picked up the bawling child, faced him nose-to-nose, and yelled, "That light is not going to turn into a monster! But *if it did,* your mother and I would keep you safe. Now go to sleep." Mom was less than pleased that her weeks of lessons on the nature of cartoons had been negated by her husband's phrase, "But if it did...." From that point on, however, everybody started sleeping again.

Clearly, the key to success lay in reassuring the child that he would be safe *no matter what.* Given that, he could then devote some energy to sorting out the differences between what was real and what wasn't. He knew all along what his parents had missed: The *character* may have been fantasy, but the *fear* was fact. Similarly, a teacher who challenges a child by asking, "What's the matter with you, can't you think?" may not be prepared to accept the answer, "No, not until I am more comfortable in this situation."

Fortunately, the opposite is also true. The brain seeks novelty, so it functions best when new and stimulating ideas and processes are presented in ways that are acceptable and appealing. There are many studies which indicate that memorization, creative output, and logical thinking all occur at peak levels when an individual is in an alert yet relaxed state.

MacLean's theory also helps us to understand why the exploration of various activities, skills, and topics should be *child*-initiated rather than adult-initiated. It is up to the parent to provide a smorgasbord of possibilities, but really intense pursuits should begin with the child. The parent who subjects a child to frequent and structured drill-and-practice should stop and think, "Who is this *really* for?" Not only is it unpleasant for the child, but it's also likely to fail due to the mechanics of the brain. Further proof of this is offered by Dr. Benjamin Bloom's study of highly successful individuals. What he found was that these achievers were all exposed to their particular fields of expertise in their early years — and then allowed to fall in love with them on their own.*

Musicians recalled that the rigor of their first musical instruction was less influential than the positive, caring attitude of their first teachers. Artists remembered that their childhood years contained little formal training but plenty of opportunities to experiment — and that most of their efforts were praised and displayed by at least one parent. While discipline and drive contributed significantly to their later success, they were not as important in the beginning, when it all took root.

The Hemispheric Specialization Model

What leads an individual child to latch onto a particular topic or process in the first place? While nobody can give a definitive answer to that question, the theory of hemispheric specialization offers some possible explanations. It is this theory that explains, to a certain extent, how the neocortex functions when conditions are right.

The neocortex is divided into two hemispheres, the left and the right. These hemispheres are connected by a large bundle of fibers called the *corpus callosum*. While each hemisphere is capable of performing most necessary activities, in a normally functioning brain each side is responsible for specific duties.

The left hemisphere largely controls the right side of the body, while the right hemisphere largely controls the left side.** The left hemisphere is the more verbal of the two and is responsible for linear and rational thinking. Reading, language, and computation are handled here. The right hemisphere, in contrast, thinks spatially, intuitively, and holistically. Mathematical concepts (e.g., geometry), metaphor, music, and visual art are the purview of this part of the brain.

---

* Benjamin Bloom, Ph.D., *Developing Talent in Young Children* (New York: Ballantine Books, Inc., 1985).

** The description which follows is accurate for most right-handed persons and for 60 percent of those who are left- handed. For the other 40 percent of left-handers, the activities of the hemispheres are reversed, but the basic ways in which activities are grouped remains the same.

There is an increasing body of evidence that autonomous, healthy, functioning individuals are those whose brain activity integrates the functions of both hemispheres. For example, problem-solving occurs most readily when an individual is able to shift as needed between left and right. Actually, almost *no* human activity is relegated solely to one hemisphere or the other, and the two hemispheres do not act independently but as parts of a whole.

Nevertheless, it appears that some individuals favor one side over the other. This preference for certain types of thinking is a factor in determining which children are predisposed to which activities. For the sake of learning, it is essential that they be exposed to activities that exercise *both* sides of the brain. The best way to approach this is by encouraging them to approach a task in a style they find comfortable, while simultaneously leaving the door open to the side of the brain they do not favor.

For example, children who tend toward an intuitive approach to solving math problems will not respond well to enforced drill-and-practice; this can only frustrate and upset them. But if they are allowed to approach math concepts and problem-solving first and the details of arithmetic later, they may flower into genuine math lovers. At some point they will have to master computation skills, but why not let them do it in a way that enhances rather than denies their natural strengths?

Enhancement is what Part II of this book is all about. However, the information offered and the strategies described can work only if they are applied in ways that suit each individual child. To impose a set theory or plan of action on a child is wrong because despite their similarities, each brain is unique. Your child's mind is more than the sum of the parts of what's inside his or her head. Being a gifted parent requires that you carefully observe your child, value your child for what he or she is *right now*, and help your child to grow according to his or her needs, not yours.

The Body-Brain Connection

It should come as no surprise that brain performance depends heavily on whole-body health, and that health depends on a balanced diet, adequate exercise, and plenty of rest. Our parents and grandparents knew as much (they're the ones who were always spouting, "A sound mind in a sound body"), and the message bears repeating in light of recent research that confirms the value of these homespun tenets as they relate to brain function.

It has been found that the brain requires specific "brain nutrients," primarily oxygen and glucose. When it comes to oxygen, the brain is the body's most avaricious organ; pound for pound, it requires ten times more O_2 than any other organ. That's why exercise and the regular pacing of sedentary with physically stimulating activity is so important to learning. The circulatory system of a 24-hour-a-day TV watcher is ill-equipped to pump to the brain the oxygen it needs.

Parents and teachers would do well to take a page from the manuals of Chinese business managers. Rather than let workers use their morning and afternoon breaks to consume caffeine-laden drinks and sugary snacks, managers encourage them to perform a vigorous pattern of physical exercises accompanied by deep breathing. This practice has been shown to reduce tension and increase productivity.

Before plunking a marginally performing child in front of the TV with an ice-cream bar and orders to "settle down," parents should consider a brisk walk or a game of tag. A child whose reptilian brain is hungry for oxygen will have an out-of-sorts limbic system, and if that child is between the ages of zero and four everyone in the vicinity will pay the price.

The other nutrient the brain needs in large quantities is glucose. Glucose is a sugar, but contrary to what seems like logic, consuming quantities of sweets won't do the trick. In fact, devouring masses of simple carbohydrates (white sugar, white flour) has the same effect on the body as spraying a charcoal fire with lighter fluid. When the lighter fluid hits the coals, there is an immediate flare-up of energy. But it doesn't last, and it doesn't subside into a steady flame; instead, the fire soon burns down lower than it was originally. Another blast of fluid is followed by another spectacular outburst and another rapid decline. Once this pattern has been set — whether in your child's digestive system or your barbecue — it's very hard to break.

Quantities of simple carbohydrates *lower* your child's blood sugar. Low blood sugar means low energy and short attention span. Low energy and short attention span mean little or no learning. It's a fairly simple equation, and one worth living by. Stand firm, even if "everyone else" in the neighborhood is allowed to eat 10-foot chocolate bunnies for breakfast.

Speaking of breakfast, yet another maxim your mother shared with you turns out to be true: Both the body and the brain function better when they are fueled by a good morning meal. "Good" can be defined as anything solid and long-lasting that the body can convert to glucose for the brain and other organs and muscles. And you don't have to stick to cornflakes. Consider peanut-butter toast on a soy-based bread, or whole-grain cereal with fruit, or even the occasional cholesterol-laden egg, all of which are high in protein and provide the lecithin and amino acids essential to the development of neurotransmitters.

For lunch, go for minerals like iron, magnesium, and zinc, which carry oxygen to the brain and can be found in those green leafy vegetables your mom was always pushing on you. If your child won't touch vegetables of any color or shape, try sneaking them into foods he or she loves (in pureed, grated, or otherwise disguised forms). Nobody has to know that the fragrant, yummy stuff wrapped in waxed paper is really zucchini bread.

In addition to exercise and food, your child's brain and body need plenty of rest. There's a widespread myth about gifted children that merits discussion here: specifically, that they need less sleep than "typical" children. This statement turns up again and again in the literature, despite the fact that various researchers have found that brighter children sleep *longer* than others.*

It is likely that the myth stemmed from two types of observations made of gifted individuals. The first was that many gifted *adults* need less sleep than the general population. Unfortunately, this was used as the jumping-off point for assuming that bright *children* are the same. This assumption was then coupled with the observation that many sensitive infants (those who are very aware of their surroundings) seem to have erratic sleep patterns which are easily disturbed. But while these infants seem to sleep less, it doesn't necessarily follow that they need less sleep.

Any parent of a fussy infant can confirm that children with a great deal of sensitivity and drive — characteristics which may later win them the label of "gifted" — may push themselves into resisting sleep, only to find themselves trapped in a pattern of chronic sleeplessness. This sleep deprivation in turn leads to a nervous-energy adrenaline output that is clearly detrimental during infancy but may be confused with "high energy" in older children and adults.

Studies have shown that adults who are running short on sleep but feeling full of energy are actually *over*stimulated. Over-stimulation leads to problems with focusing, attending to task, and sorting out detail.

The bottom line is that any brain — young or old, "superior" or not — runs best when it has had enough rest. Although the precise quantity varies from individual to individual, don't let your child bamboozle you into believing that he or she needs less than a sensible amount. It simply isn't true. Generally speaking, a child who doesn't sleep is a child who has never formed good sleeping habits. Helping your child to do so is part of your job as a parent.

---

* Mark Weissbluth, M.D., writing in the *Gifted Children Monthly* (December 1985), cites Lewis Terman (1925), Japanese researchers (1927), and Canadian researchers (1982), all of whom arrived at this conclusion after studying groups of gifted children and those with better grades.

For months, six-year-old Melanie insisted that she "wasn't tired" at bedtime. She made such a fuss that Mom and Dad finally decided to let her read herself to sleep. They figured that they'd be up late enough to turn off her light and tuck her in.

No such luck. The first night, Melanie stayed up past midnight; the second, until nearly 1 a.m. She finally settled into a pattern of falling asleep at around 11:30.

Toward the end of the week, Melanie's teacher sent a note home with her, asking what on earth was going on. The normally well-behaved little girl was grumpy and aggressive. She wouldn't pay attention in class. She didn't want to do the work. She wasn't cooperating, period.

That was enough for Melanie's parents. They laid down the law: No more reading in bed. Melanie was between the sheets at 7:55, and the lights went out at 8:00 sharp. She yelled, she protested, she sang, she talked to herself, she threatened to stay awake all night, she got up to go to the bathroom at least nine times. Mom and Dad sat reading in the living room, gritting their teeth and ignoring the clamor that came from Melanie's room.

It took nearly two more weeks, but things finally calmed down. Melanie started falling asleep at around 8:30. And her teacher was pleased to report that her problem behaviors had subsided.

Recommended Reading

If you want to know more about the brain, read:

The Brain Book by Peter Russell (New York: E.P. Dutton, Inc.,
    1979).

Left Brain, Right Brain by Sally P. Springer and Georg Deutsch
    (New York: W.H. Freeman, 1985).

The Mind by Anthony Smith (New York: Viking Press, 1984).

If you want to know more about the body-brain connection, read:

Eating Your Way Through Life by Judith J. Wurtman, Ph.D. (New
    York: Raven Press, 1979).

Child of Mine: Feeding with Love and Good Sense by Ellyn Satler
    (Palo Alto, California: Bull Publishing, 1983).

Grow Healthy Kids! by Linda Peavy and Andrea Pagenkopf (New
    York: Grosset and Dunlap, 1980).

Crybabies by Mark Weissbluth (New York: Arbor House, 1984).
    Describes in detail how parents can influence a child's sleep
    habits.

CHAPTER 5

Activities to Do with Your Child

T here are many advantages to having an arsenal of activities to do with your child. For one, it helps to maintain the sanity of the adults in the house by quieting cries of "I DON'T HAVE ANYTHING TO DO!" For another, it ensures that your child will get the kinds of experience that provide a good base for continuing growth. For a third, it gives you several ways to respond to and nurture your child's special abilities.

The following guidelines should prove useful as you develop quality activities for your child:

1. Keep them as freewheeling as your own nature and home environment will allow. Like the rest of us, young children learn best when they're having a good time. Overly structured activities can smother a child's sense of fun. All you really need are consistent rules regarding safety and respect for others, and plenty of room to move within these rules.

Given the complex schedules of today's families and the restrictions imposed by contemporary urban life, modern children do not have available to them the range of activities most of us grew up with. Fewer still can roam their communities like young Tom Sawyers and Huck Finns. In the past, a child left to his or her own devices was virtually assured of accumulating a wealth of experiences over time. In the 1980s, even three- and four-year-old children can get in a rut of watching the same TV programs and playing in the same limited space day after day.

This poses a quandary for us as parents. We want our children to benefit from a variety of spontaneous learning activities, but we find it necessary to structure the things they do. We know that quality activities should be child-initiated, but we also feel the need to steer our kids in the right direction.

Here's where the second guideline comes in:

2. Offer your child a wide range of options from which to choose. A child's week should be a relaxed smorgasbord of delights to sample. It's up to us to provide a balanced menu, but it should be left to the child to make the selections. Not only will this result in a well-fed mind; it may also spark the desire to pursue a specific choice to the point of becoming a gourmet in the field. How will a four-year-old learn that he loves to dance if he is never exposed to music and movement? How will a five-year-old discover a talent for composing if she never has access to a musical instrument? While it isn't appropriate to force young children into formalized learning experiences in *every* field, it's fine to tempt them with possibilities.

Which leads to the third guideline:

3. Make sure that the activities require hands-on, total involvement on the part of the child. Studies have shown that the more involved a person becomes in a specific activity or pursuit, the more parts of the brain come into play. Listening involves only a small percentage of the brain; looking, a bit more; and writing, more still. But none of these approaches the kind of exercise the brain receives when the intellect, emotions, senses, and muscles are called on to work together. This is especially significant for young children, since the neural connections necessary for sophisticated thinking are still being formed at this age.

Experts in the field of writing stress the importance of oral expression and body language over letter formation as key to the later development of writing skill. Many math educators prefer that children not do math problems on paper until age eight, but instead practice with manipulatives — blocks, puzzles, beads, geometric shapes — that lead to an understanding of concepts.

> **WARNING:**
> **EDUCATIONAL ACTIVITIES MAY BE HAZARDOUS TO YOUR CHILD'S MENTAL HEALTH**

Included on these pages are several activities to try with your child. You may be surprised to find that many do not seem "educational" at all. In fact, so-called "educational activities" may be hazardous to your child's mental health and whole attitude toward learning.

Even though most parents are intuitively aware that spontaneity, variety, and involvement are what children need most in order to learn, it's easy for a conscientious parent to get sucked into programs long on surface appeal and short on substance. While there's little harm in letting a child do some pages in a "math readiness" workbook purchased at a grocery store — *as long as the child wants to* — there isn't much value in it, either. That time could be much better spent in interdisciplinary pursuits. And it goes without saying that if the child *doesn't* want to do the workbook, and the parent insists on it anyway, serious damage could be done to the child's perceptions of the learning process.

The requirements for the job of stocking supermarket shelves don't yet include a degree in early childhood development or education. Better you should trust your own instincts regarding what your child will benefit from and enjoy; say no to the current mania for forcing kids into unnatural academic configurations before they are ready. Packaged "programs" sell not because they're based on sound educational theory, but because they pander to the anxieties of parents who want to be sure to give their children all of the "proper" advantages.

The following activities incorporate educational principles without belaboring the point. They are loosely grouped by categories — not to imply that you should provide your child with "study time" in each area, but to give you several topics from which to choose.

Finally, our lists are by no means conclusive. Use them as starting-points for exploring other activities — or creating your own.

Language Activities

Most children don't need to be "taught" basic language skills. They naturally assimilate them during the first three to five years of life. This is not to imply that learning the language is easy; in fact, it's an incredibly complex process. But even small children routinely apply the many rules of grammar, syntax, and usage. "Errors" in their speech often reflect a very sophisticated understanding of the principles of language usage. The child who says, "I bringed you a flower," is forming the past tense of "to bring" in a way that is consistent with most English verbs.

Language development is not completely automatic, however. Verbally proficient persons (children and adults) tend to come from homes in which language is used creatively and constantly. They master it because they have been immersed in all its facets since birth. Although individual children seem to be born with a greater or lesser aptitude for language development, the environment *always* has a significant impact.

Consider a pair of two-year-olds from different families. Both spill their milk. One chants "boo-boo, boo-boo" while waiting for an adult to show up with a towel; the other shouts, "Crisis, Mom, crisis!" Obviously there are differences in both innate ability and experience.

For children whose talents lie elsewhere (perhaps in spatial or mathematical areas), appropriate language stimulation is needed for them to become efficient users of the tools of speech. For children with a bent for verbal communication, an enriched language environment will give wings to their ability.

In our culture, language and thought are inextricably linked. Certainly there are important thoughts that occur nonverbally, but for the most part the power of ideas is related to the language used to express them. A mastery of the language brings with it the joys of clarifying and communicating one's thoughts in precise, imaginative, influential, even graceful ways. An inspiring speech, a moving appeal, a delicate lyric, a poet's turn of phrase — all are products of knowing how and when, why and where to use *this* word rather than *that* one, or *this* inflection instead of another.

When concerning yourself with your child's language development, keep in mind two basic goals of early language learning:

1. First and foremost, children should feel comfortable expressing themselves. This means that when your child speaks, you should try to listen attentively. Show that you're listening by responding appropriately — although we're all guilty of the occasional "uh-huh...uh-huh..." in answer to a never-ending story or a joke that goes nowhere.

Offer corrections only where appropriate, and do it subtly. Work the correct usage into the conversation without belaboring the child's mistake in grammar or pronunciation. For example, in response to "I bringed you a flower," you might say, "Thank you. You brought me a flower."

2. Second, children need to be encouraged to recognize language use as a vehicle for expression, both within themselves and with others. This has some very practical applications. For example, it's far preferable for a child to tell a friend, "I don't like it when you take my toys," than for the child to haul off and whack the offending playmate.

Parents of gifted children especially need to stay focused on these two goals. With countless activity books and home-teaching manuals stressing vocabulary building, reading, and letter formation, it's easy to confuse the means with the end. The child who learns to love the richness of language and feels empowered by its use will be motivated to master the details in due time. The child who is subjected to drill-and-practice in letter formation may decide that communication is a laborious and unrewarding task.

High-potential children present distinct challenges in this area. Regardless of their degree of language proficiency, their minds are ready to race on to the next step. Such children often want explanations for specific phenomena but lack the vocabulary or abstract reasoning skills needed to fully understand the explanations.

Then there are those who recognize that reading and writing are the keys to an "older" world. They are desperate to master them but lack the necessary fine-motor coordination and/or attention span. As a parent, you can create activities promoting specific reading and writing skills that complement your child's emotional needs and stage of development.

Good language activities for bright young children share the following characteristics:

* *They encourage, through modeling and practice, the rich, colorful, and precise use of words*
* *They neither push nor patronize the child.*
* *They encourage many forms of expression through the use of body language, facial expression, and noise as well as words.* This lays the groundwork for the development of the intuitive sense that different forms of communication are appropriate in different settings. It's as important to exercise the mind and body as it is to exercise the tongue. Even such a small thing as saying, "You're jumping for joy, aren't you?" helps a child to categorize this action as a form of communication.
* *They offer the child a varied and legitimate audience for his or her attempts to communicate.* The whole point of language is communication. The more audiences a child has on which to practice these skills, the more developed they will become. Good language activities give children feedback from people they care about — parents, teachers, grandparents, other authority figures.

It's important to recognize that children need practice in failed and successful communication alike in order to internalize the components of both and be able to tell them apart. This means resisting the temptation to put words in your child's mouth while he or she is talking. For example, if your child asks the librarian for "a book on flying things" when what he or she really wants is a book on pterodactyls, let your child and the librarian work it out together, even if you know precisely what your child has in mind. It may take time, but your child will learn the need to phrase such a request as precisely as possible.

• *They recognize that it is harder to generate language than to receive it.* Although listening is an important skill, any learning activity is enhanced when your child listens for a purpose and is able to do something with the information he or she receives. This is one reason why too much television — even "educational" television — is counterproductive to the advancement of real communication skills.

Suggested Home Activities

Get a double set of magnetic letters (so your choice of messages is not limited to only one word containing the letter C) and leave

short, personal messages to your child on the refrigerator door.
See whether your child can spell one or more words using the
letters of the original message.

Make a game of memorizing children's poems together.
Possible sources include:

Where the Sidewalk Ends (New York: Harper & Row, 1974) and
   The Light in the Attic (New York: Harper & Row, 1981) by Shel
   Silverstein.

Poem Stew (New York: J.B. Lippincott, 1983). This is an assort-
   ment of poems selected by William Cole. Featured poets include Ogden Nash, John Ciardi, Richard Armour, X.J. Ken-
   nedy, and our old friend Anonymous.

The Nonsense Verse of Edward Lear (New York: Harmony Books,
   1984). Some of these are rather sophisticated, but many are
   fun. Even "The Owl and the Pussycat" is manageable by
   young children; if they can't handle the whole thing, try just a
   verse or two.

Don't think you have to stick to poetry written expressly for
children. Many so-called "adult" poets are also accessible. Some
collections have been arranged for children and colorfully illustrated besides. Try:

I'm Nobody! Who Are You? Poems of Emily Dickinson for Children
Under the Greenwood Tree: Shakespeare for Young People
A Swinger of Birches: Poems of Robert Frost for Young People
All are published by Stemmer House in Owings Mills, Maryland.

Again, it's sometimes enough to memorize a verse or a couplet.

There are many benefits to be gained from teaching your
child to memorize early in life. Perhaps the most important is that
it enables you to get the jump on the teacher who uses memorization as a punishment or a disciplinary tactic. Most adults today
can remember being forced to memorize and recite verses; no
wonder so many of us grew up hating poetry!

One mom was able to teach her three-year-old several poems
after first delivering this introduction: "Jamie, once you memorize
something, it belongs to you forever. You can think it or say it
whenever you want. You don't have to wait for me or Daddy to

read it to you. Even if you lose the book, you will still have the poem. Now, which poem would you like to have as your very own?"

Finally, if you have any abilities whatsoever in this area, make up poems for your child. If they incorporate his or her name, so much the better. Verses can be used to commemorate special occasions — or to deal with specific concerns or fears. Another mom made up a chant for her four-year-old to say whenever he became afraid of the dark.

Work together to make bright, colorful labels for appliances and objects in the kitchen. It may give the area a slightly surrealistic look, but it's worth it in the late afternoon when dinner needs attention and the child is begging, "Play with me!" You can then resort to variations of a spelling game and keep on cooking. When simple questions like "How do you spell stove?" begin to lose their charm, you can move on to, "Find something that chops up food and starts with a B. Right, now how do you spell blender?"

Offer to label any drawings your child makes (but never insist that your offer be accepted). Write *exactly* what the child says in precisely the way he or she wants it. This reinforces the perception that words and letters are symbols, and also shows respect for the child's use of language.

Provide the child with an audience for his or her work. This is one of the underlying philosophies of teaching writing. Consider mailing drawings, labeled illustrations, and short notes to the child's favorite people. Mail carriers — and, for that matter, all aspects of the postal system — are powerful stuff to many small children, and writing to Grandma (even if she lives close enough for frequent calls and visits) gives an aura of importance and value to written forms of communication.

Try a treasure hunt on a rainy day. Hide a favorite toy or treat. Then write on 3x5 cards (or pieces of paper) clues that combine words and pictures. A typical clue might be a picture of a ball with the word "ball" printed next to it and a question mark following. On the back could be a picture of a chair. The object of this treasure hunt is a ball, and the clue indicates where the child might find the next clue leading to it.

For small children, three to four clues are enough. For children of any age, you'd best be prepared with clues for at least one more round; this activity is usually a big hit.

Use chalk to draw a huge circle or square on a sidewalk or driveway and divide it into four to six parts. Write a letter in each part. Then play a variation of "Simon Says" in which Simon issues orders such as, "Jump up and down on the S" or "Wiggle all over the letter that says 'sssssss.'"

This is especially recommended for children who are begging to learn letters and sounds but are frustrated because they are unable or unwilling to sit still for alphabet books.

Expose your child to many different types of music. Music relates to language in that it is a form of communication, but it has an even more specific correlation to language development. Rhythmic music and chanting develop in a child a sense of the rhythm and cadence inherent to language. (The Reverend Jesse Jackson makes brilliant use of these elements in his speeches.)

Provide opportunities for sequencing. How well your child writes in the coming years will depend on his or her ability to put a series of thoughts in logical order. Use this activity as a starting point: Cut apart some of your child's favorite comic strips and ask him or her to place them in the proper story-telling sequence. Nonreaders will use the pictures as clues; readers will use the text. Encourage your reader to go a step further by blacking out the text and asking the child to first sequence the panels and then write captions to fit the sequence.

Play word games that give practice in going from the general to the specific. You say "bug," your child says "ant." You say "liquid," your child lists as many types of liquids as possible.

Use magazine pictures to create a rebus. A rebus is a story or message that uses both words and pictures. For example: "A 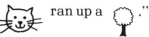 ran up a 🌳."

It usually works best to start with a group of pictures and then try to write a story around them. It can be frustrating for a small child to attempt to go the other way (starting with a story first, searching for pictures second).

Mount rebus stories on sturdy backing for the child to "read" again and again.

Play a variation of the alphabet game in which words must fit certain categories. For example, "Name a person, an animal, and a toy that begin with the letter A.... Now name a person, an animal, and a toy that begin with the letter B...."

Answer questions about word meanings with trips to the dictionary — and have your child help to look up definitions. You should have on hand at least one good children's dictionary. Try either (or both) of these:

My First Dictionary: An American Heritage Dictionary (Boston: Houghton Mifflin, 1980).

Macmillan Very First Dictionary: A Magic World of Words (New York: Macmillan Publishing Co., Inc., 1983).

Both are liberally illustrated and contain not only simple definitions but also sample sentences.

□ ■ □

Because you're dealing with a bright child, you can also experiment with activities that are off the beaten path. Make them available, then let your child decide whether to pursue them.

The mother of six-year-old Joshua reads to him in Latin — at his request. It all started with a discussion about evolution. Joshua had seen a picture of a woolly mammoth and wanted to know if there were any at the local zoo. Mom said no, but there were elephants, and elephants were the great-great-great-great-great (etc.) grandchildren of woolly mammoths. Then she casually mentioned that words evolved, too. Joshua wanted some examples, so Mom dug into her memories of long-ago high-school Latin. When Joshua asked to hear more, Mom hauled out a dusty copy of Ovid's *Metamorphoses* and read aloud from it for a few minutes. Since then, Joshua occasionally asks if she'll do it again, and Mom obliges.

Which leads to another important point: If at all possible, give your child some exposure to languages other than English. Kids can quickly master the accents and inflections of a foreign tongue; if you speak a second language, do so around your child.

You may want to follow the practice of some bilingual families who speak a foreign language at home and English everywhere else.

Even if you know only a few simple words or phrases of Spanish or Italian or French or Serbo-Croation or any other language, teach them to your child — almost as you would a short poem. This accomplishes several purposes: It acquaints the child with the fact that there are many ways of saying the same thing; it may spark a propensity for languages; and it helps to develop the beginnings of a global perspective.

We've met five-year-olds who are fascinated by etymology and a three-year-old who can spout Hungarian, French, and Polish phrases (thanks to a multilingual daycare mom). These are children who delight in language, and they're a delight to be around.

Should You Teach Your Child to Read?

Together with early entrance (see Chapter 10), the teaching of reading to preschool children is one of the most controversial topics in education today. Proponents argue
— that early education is effective,
— that parents know their children best and, as a result, make the best teachers, and
— that to delay reading instruction is to waste valuable educational time.

Meanwhile, opponents express concern
— that a young child must make an enormous psychological investment to master such a complex task,
— that amateur reading teachers (such as parents) are likely to make costly mistakes, and
— that the child will subsequently be bored in school when reading instruction is redundant.

While each side raises some valid issues, both seem to miss a crucial point: *There is a big difference between learning to read and becoming a reader.* Over 90 percent of the American adult population is considered to be literate, but only 16 percent read one or more books a year.

Given this frightening fact, the first priority of parents and preschool educators should be to develop in children *positive attitudes toward and feelings about reading*. They should make reading so attractive that when children are ready to read, they will choose to do so. Children become readers not because they *can* read, but because they *want* to read and *do* read.

In other words, don't force your child to read. It's okay to encourage your child with small treats or rewards (for example, a sticker on completing a book, or membership in a Library Club), but the moment reading seems like drudgery, stop. Don't insist that your child perform for others; if he or she wants to read aloud to playmates or a younger sibling, that's fine, but it's not fair to demand that a show be put on for Grandpa.

When one has a gifted child and knows it, it's always tempting to see the child as a reflection of oneself and one's parenting abilities. Our most well-intentioned wishes for our children can easily get confused with our own egos. That's why it's wise to pause on occasion to take stock of our motives. Do we want our children to read early because it will make *us* look good? Or do we want them to read early because we're eager for them to discover the joys that reading can bring? (Even this latter seemingly generous urge can be a trap. There's no guarantee that our children will like the same things we do.)

You can rest assured that your child will eventually learn to read, one way or another. If it doesn't happen before school, it will happen in school. At this stage, your best approach is to leave the door open by providing your child with positive pre-reading experiences.

Incidentally, this approach is in keeping with the brain-development theories discussed earlier. A child who comes away from pre-reading activities with the feeling that reading is a good thing to do will have a limbic system that enhances rather than inhibits the cortex when it's time to begin formal instruction.

Brain research has also shown that the pre-frontal lobes of the cortex do not fully close until somewhere between the ages of four and eight. Closure is necessary for a child to become a fluent reader. It occurs at varying rates in individual children, and *it has nothing to do with ability*. While some gifted children do read very early, as many as 80 percent of children currently in school programs for the gifted were not yet reading at the time they started school.

Nancy Polette, author of many highly respected books and activity units on teaching reading to gifted children,* maintains that "Reading is a lifestyle as much as a skill." She recommends that any teacher of young children, parent or professional, establish the following two goals for early reading experiences:

1. The experiences should develop in the child a love of language, and

2. The experiences should set the stage for appropriate process development.

You can help to ensure that when your child's brain is physiologically ready for reading (and other types of structured thinking), he or she will move ahead smoothly and enthusiastically.

□ ■ □

There are several strategies known to encourage a positive attitude toward reading. The most obvious of these is simply to *model reading behavior*. There is no, repeat *no*, better way to instill a driving curiosity about reading in your child than by doing it your-

---

* See, for example, her *Picture Books for Gifted Programs* (Metuchen, New Jersey: Scarecrow Press, 1981).

self frequently, by choice, and with evident pleasure. Most of what you read probably won't be suitable for reading aloud, but you may want to share an occasional idea that you think your child might enjoy discussing. Make it clear that the source of the idea was something you read, and point out the particular article or book.

> "One factor educators agree on is that parental modeling of reading skills, as well as availability of reading materials in the home, has a big impact on encouraging the early reader." Sheila C. Perino and Joseph Perino, *Parenting the Gifted: Developing the Promise* (New York: R.R. Bowker, 1981), p. 27.

A house full of things to read is another clear sign that you value reading and derive something positive from it. We both grew up around plenty of books, and our children are doing the same today. And our books aren't always neatly organized on shelves, either. They're heaped on bedside tables, lined up on fireplace mantles, and sometimes piled on the floor. They're treated with respect, but this isn't carried to extremes. We make it clear that books aren't to be scribbled in or dribbled on, but we leave them around to be paged through by little fingers as well as big ones, and we allow for occasional accidents.

Even more important than modeling reading behavior is to *read aloud to your child*. This has been shown to have a direct effect on a child's future as a reader. (Interestingly, it often happens that preschoolers who learn to read conceal this fact from their parents, fearing that their parents will stop reading to them once they can do it themselves!) The best time to start is in infancy. The best time to stop may be never. Some parents read to their children all the way up to their teens.

What should you read to your young child? The answer to that question is wide open. Many parents, however — including those who read voraciously — feel stumped when it comes to choosing books for their kids. One mother who's both a reader and a writer remembers the day she went shopping for "first books" for her still unborn child. She came home with a sack full of Little Golden Books because she remembered them from her childhood.

A good way to begin educating yourself about children's literature is by talking with the children's librarian at your local branch library. In general, librarians are eager to show off their personal favorites. It's their job to keep current on what's being published, and they have an inside track on which books are best loved by children and their parents.

Best Bet Authors

When we asked parents what books they read to their children, the same authors' names came up over and over again. Although this list is by no means definitive — in fact, it barely scratches the surface of what's available today — it can move you in the direction of books that are bound to please and are recognized as being high in both verbal and visual quality:

Peter Spier • Mercer Mayer • Maurice Sendak • Beverly Cleary • Aliki • Arnold Lobel • Chris Van Allsburg • William Steig • Judith Viorst • Nancy Carlson • Else Holmelund Minarik • Beatrix Potter • Mitsumasa Anno • A.A. Milne • Tomie dePaola • Harry Allard • James Marshall • Peggy Parish • Marc Brown • Lillian and Russel Hoban • Tana Hoban • James Stevenson • Jane Yolen • Anne Rockwell

Most children's libraries schedule special events — puppet shows, film festivals, bedtime story hours. Children love the story hours, and so do parents; they're terrific entertainment, and they're free. It's even more fun when the kids show up in their pajamas with stuffed animals tucked under their arms. (Sometimes the adult storyteller will wear pajamas, too.)

When you decide to start building a home library, you can't go wrong with any of the following:

The two-volume *World Treasury of Children's Literature*, selected and with commentary by Clifton Fadiman (Boston: Little, Brown and Company, 1984).

This spectacular collection offers 140 traditional and modern favorites from around the world — Margaret Wise Brown's *Goodnight Moon*, H.A. Rey's *Curious George*, Jean de Brunhoff's *The Story of Babar the Elephant*, countless poems, fairy tales, myths, fables...almost anything you might want to read to your child. Its only shortcoming is due to space considerations, which didn't permit the inclusion of every original illustration. But you can always back up a first reading of, for example, Munro Leaf's *The Story of Ferdinand* with a trip to the library to see all the pictures.

Books that bear the gold-embossed Caldecott Medal or the silver-embossed Caldecott Honor Seal.

The Caldecott awards are given annually for the most distinguished American children's books. Winners are chosen by the Children's Services Division of the American Library Association. Check with your librarian for a complete list. Then stop by your bookstore; many now stock the most recent Caldecott winners, and some are being made available in paperback.

Weekly library visits should become part of your regular family routine. Let your child play an active role in deciding which books to bring home. Those that get renewed more than once may be good candidates for your home library.

One way to make reading aloud an especially worthwhile activity for your child is to borrow from the philosophy and techniques of *bibliotherapy*. Bibliotherapy uses books as jumping-off points for discussing emotional and psychological issues important to the reader's (or listener's) life. This has added value for young children in that the resulting discussions can help them to cope with their ever-changing selves, as well as imparting to them the sense that reading is emotionally satisfying.

Listed below are some titles that parents have described as particularly interesting and useful. They are arranged by topics that tend to be germane to the lives of bright young children. For example, you might use the books under the "Individual Differences" heading to initiate conversations about your child's unique capabilities, how it feels to be different from other children, and why it's important to try to understand the feelings and motivations of others.

CAUTION: A little guided discussion goes a long way.

Don't overdo it with your child. And when he or she wants to change the subject, don't insist on continuing until you've had your say.

Books That Address Issues

Individual Differences

Just Like Everyone Else by Karla Kuskin (New York: Harper & Row, 1982). Jonathon James appears to be like everyone else — until the surprising last page.

Making the Team by Nancy Carlson (Minneapolis: Carolrhoda Books, 1985). Louanne the pig and Arnie the cat find that they are most successful when they use their own talents and ignore sex-role stereotypes.

I Love Every-People by Florence Parry Heide and Roxanne Heide; illustrated by John Sanford (St. Louis, Missouri: Concordia Publishing House, 1978). A celebration of individual differences in a religious context. Original, witty illustrations.

Leo the Late Bloomer by Robert Kraus (New York: T.Y. Crowell, 1971). Leo the Lion has trouble eating neatly, etc. Mom is confident that Leo will "bloom" eventually.

Thy Friend, Obadiah by Brinton Turkle (New York: Viking, 1969). Young Obadiah, a Quaker in Nantucket, is embarrassed at being singled out by a seagull. Evocative text and illustrations.

War and Conflict

The Butter Battle Book by Dr. Seuss (New York: Random House, 1984). No easy solutions are found when neighboring communities escalate their weaponry in an argument over which side of bread should be buttered.

On Being Gifted

The Gifted Kids Survival Guide (For Ages 10 & Under) by Judy Galbraith (Minneapolis: Free Spirit Publishing, 1984). An excellent resource to keep on hand as your child reaches seven or eight years old.

Starting School ~~~~~~~~~~~~~~~~~~~~~~~~~~~~

Fred's First Day by Cathy Warren, illustrated by Pat Cummings (New York: Lothrop, Lee & Shepard Books, 1984). Fred's first day at preschool is traumatic but successful.

Ramona the Pest by Beverly Cleary (New York: Dell/Yearling, 1968). Not a picture book, but a wonderful and entertaining story centering around the precocious Ramona Quimby's kindergarten experiences.

Death, Loss, and Aging ~~~~~~~~~~~~~~~~~~~~

The Tenth Good Thing About Barney by Judith Viorst, illustrated by Erik Blegvad (New York: Atheneum Press, 1983). A sensitive handling of a boy's reaction to the death of his cat.

The Black Dog Who Went Into the Wood by Edith Thatcher Hurd (New York: Harper & Row, 1980). Family reactions to the death of a dog.

How Does It Feel To Be Old? by Norma Farber (New York: E.P. Dutton, 1979). An elderly woman describes to a child how it feels to be old. Fine poetry and illustrations.

The Two of Them by Aliki (New York: Greenwillow Books, 1979). A nicely handled story of the love between a child and a grandfather.

Emotions ~~~~~~~~~~~~~~~~~~~~~~~~~~~~~~~~~~

The Temper Tantrum Book by Edna Mitchell Preston, illustrated by Rainey Bennett (New York: Penguin Books, 1969). Young animals stomp, howl, and squeal in response to haircombing, napping, and the like.

The Silver Pony by Lynd Ward (Boston: Houghton-Mifflin, 1973). A farm boy uses flights of fancy to combat his loneliness and isolation.

If I Were in Charge of the World and Other Worries by Judith Viorst (New York: Atheneum Press, 1981). Humorous and touching poems about anxiety and other feelings.

Sweet Dreams for Little Ones by Michael Pappas (Minneapolis: Winston Press, 1982). Creative imagery exercises to use at bedtime. Each helps children gain confidence and self-esteem.

Troubled Times ~~~~~~~~~~~~~~~~~~~~~~~~~~~~~~~~~~

Oops by Mercer Mayer (New York: Dial Press, 1977). A wordless
   book about a charming lady hippo who wreaks accidental
   havoc.

Alexander and the Terrible, Horrible, No Good, Very Bad Day by
   Judith Viorst, illustrated by Ray Cruz (New York: Atheneum
   Press, 1972). Alexander suffers through the kind of day no
   one should have but everyone eventually does.

Benjamin and Tulip by Rosemary Wells (New York: Dial Press,
   1973). Benjamin the raccoon suffers at the hand of bully Tulip.
   Text and illustrations show wit and zest.

□ ■ □

Although reading something is almost always preferable to reading nothing, the better the books you read to your child, the more
likely he or she will learn to intuitively recognize the richness
books can bring to life. A library chosen on impulse at the supermarket won't hurt your child, but neither will it have the same
impact.

When choosing books for your child, keep the following questions in mind:

• *Will the book truly appeal to your child, or is it just some
adult's idea (maybe yours!) of what your child might like?*

• *Does the book have substance? Or does it rely on TV characters or visual gimmicks for appeal?*

• *Does it speak to children at their level without patronizing
them?*

• *Does it offer something new by way of concept development,
values clarification, humor, or aesthetic appreciation?*

• *Are visuals and text of equally high quality?* In a society where
most role models for visual expression are limited to TV programs, billboards, and advertisements, high-quality art in picture
books provides a vital antidote.

• *Does it contain any hidden messages that you don't want your
child to receive?* Consider the impact of the seemingly innocuous
version of Little Red Riding Hood that ends "and she never was

curious and naughty again." Watch also for sexism; while most authors and publishers these days are conscious of the need to avoid sex-role stereotyping in language, illustrations, and story lines, some do little more than dress an occasional character in a skirt. And, finally,

• *Do YOU like the book?* You may end up reading it dozens, maybe hundreds of times over the next few years. Are you prepared to become intimate with its contents while exhibiting continued enthusiasm (or at least good grace)?

Books on Tape

A fairly recent alternative available to parents and children is the recorded book on audiocassette. Books on tape are becoming increasingly popular, which means that more and more titles are being made available. Among our favorites are Carol Channing's readings of the works of Maurice Sendak — with Mozart's music in the background.

Any good toy store, as well as some bookstores, will have a decent selection in stock. Or write for a catalog to: Caedmon Spoken Word Records and Cassettes, 1995 Broadway, New York, NY 10023.

While nothing can replace a parent's lap for comfort, and taped books don't have pictures, there are times when these are ideal — including long car trips and occasions when Mom and Dad would prefer Junior to entertain himself for a while somewhere besides in front of the TV. If you don't want your child using the family stereo system, consider a small, sturdy child's tape player, such as the Fisher-Price.

□ ■ □

If it's evident that your child *wants* to read early, there are ways to encourage this in addition to simply providing plenty of books. Here are some techniques parents have found effective:

• **Make your child a part of your reading rituals.** Perhaps you read in a certain room and sit in a certain chair. Invite the child to be part of this group by adding a comfortable kid-sized chair and maybe even a small table and reading lamp.

• **Set aside a shelf in a bookcase for the exclusive use of your child, or provide an entire bookcase in his or her room.**

• **Let your child have his or her own library card.** In many libraries, the only requirement is that the child be able to sign his or her name.

• **Try to establish a time each day that's devoted to reading — reading aloud to your child, or having your child read aloud to you, or reading your own books side-by-side.** One family has made Friday nights special by allowing their child to stay up as late as he likes — as long as he's in bed reading. And he's allowed to take to bed any book in the house he's interested in perusing. Usually he retires with an armload of picture books, but sometimes he chooses magazines, art museum catalogs, or a dictionary. He genuinely looks forward to his weekly treat, and his parents have a peaceful evening together!

• **Buy a child-sized backpack and encourage your child to bring a book or two along on trips to the doctor, to visit friends, wherever.**

• **Get in the habit of turning to books whenever your child asks questions you can't answer off the top of your head.** ("What is soap made of?" "How tall is the Empire State Building?" "What do butterflies eat?") One dad writes down the questions his five-year-old daughter asks throughout the week, and then they troop off to the library together each Saturday afternoon to do "research."

Listed below are some books parents have turned to for answers to the endless questions of their preschoolers. Because

they have been written for children, the explanations they provide are in language that kids can understand. Each, of course,
may also be used to spark a child's interest in a particular topic.

Books That Answer Questions

General

All published by Random House (New York):

> *Charlie Brown's Super Book of Questions and Answers About All
> Kinds of Animals from Snails to People* (1976)
> *Charlie Brown's Second Super Book of Questions and Answers:
> About Earth and Space from Plants to Planets* (1977)
> *Charlie Brown's Third Book of Questions and Answers: About All
> Kinds of Boats and Trains, Cars and Planes and Other Things That
> Move* (1978)
> *Charlie Brown's Fourth Book of Questions and Answers: About All
> Kinds of People and How They Live* (1979)
> *Charlie Brown's Fifth Book of Questions and Answers: About All
> Kinds of Things and How They Work* (1981)

All by Eliot Humberstone and published by EDC Publishing (Tulsa,
Oklahoma):

> *Things That Go* (1981)
> *Things Outdoors* (1981)
> *Things At Home* (1981)

The "Let's Find Out" series, by various authors and published by
Franklin Watts, Inc. (New York).

The "Wonders of the World" series, by various authors and published by Troll Associates (Mahwah, New Jersey), including:

> *Discovering the Stars* by Laurence Santrey (1982)
> *What Makes It Rain?* by Keith Brandt (1982)
> *Wonders of the Desert* by Louis Sabin (1982)

The "Creative's Little Question Books" series, by various authors
and published by Creative Education, Inc. (Mankato, MN).

Books by Gail Gibbons and published by Crowell Junior Books (New York), including:

> *Trucks* (1981)
> *New Road!* (1983)
> *Fire! Fire!* (1984)

History/Biography

Books by Jean Fritz and published by Coward, McCann, and Geoghegan, part of the Putnam Publishing Group (New York), including:

> *What's the Big Idea, Ben Franklin* (1976)
> *And Then What Happened, Paul Revere?* (1973)
> *Where Do You Think You're Going, Christopher Columbus?* (1980)

Plants and Animals

Books by Ruth Heller and published by G.P. Putnam's Sons (New York), including:

> *Chickens Aren't the Only Ones* (1981). What do lizards, chickens, and turtles have in common?
> *Animals Born Alive and Well* (1982)
> *The Reason for a Flower* (1983)
> *Plants that Never Ever Bloom* (1984)

Geography

Books by Imelda and Robert Updegraff, published by Penguin, and distributed by Puffin Books, Inc. (New York):

> *Continents and Climates* (1983)
> *Earthquakes and Volcanos* (1983)
> *Mountains and Valleys* (1983)
> *Seas and Oceans* (1983)
> *Weather* (1983)

Prehistoric Creatures

Books by Aliki and published by Harper & Row (New York):

> *Fossils Tell of Long Ago* (1972)
> *My Visit to the Dinosaurs* (1976)
> *Wild and Wooly Mammoths* (1977)

The Human Body ~~~~~~~~~~~~~~~~~~~~~~~~~~~~~~~~~~~~~~~

What Happens to a Hamburger? by Paul Showers (New York: Harper & Row, 1962)

The Skeleton Inside You by Philip Balestrino (New York: Harper & Row, 1971)

Bodies by Barbara Brenner (New York: E.P. Dutton, 1973)

Faces by Barbara Brenner (New York: E.P. Dutton, 1970)

Space ~~~~~~

The NOVA Space Explorer's Guide (New York: Clarkson Potter, distributed by Crown Publishers, Inc., 1985). Takes young readers on a thrilling rocket trip through the solar system. Many photos from NASA.

The Children's Book and Music Center is an excellent source for books and records that may be hard to find outside specialty shops. To request a copy of their catalog, write: Children's Book and Music Center, 2500 Santa Monica Blvd., Santa Monica, CA 90404. Or call 1 (800) 443-1856; in California, call (213) 829-0215.

□ ■ □

Recall Nancy Polette's recommendation that pre-reading experiences set the stage for appropriate process development. This means providing your child with the opportunity to practice processes that are necessary to fluent reading and reasoning.

Jean Piaget, pioneer explorer of how children think, defined four basic periods in the development of cognitive processes: *sensory-motor* (from 0-24 months), *pre-operational* (from 2-7 years), *concrete operational* (from 7-11 years), and *formal operational* (8 years and older, if at all).

Between the ages of four and eight or nine, most children begin to move from the pre-operational to the concrete operational stage. It is during this transition period that the child progresses from reasoning based solely on observation to applying logic in conjunction with those observations. According to Piaget, this is a natural progression that occurs when the child reaches a certain maturation point — and not before. In other words, it is not possible to teach a child to move from one stage to the next.

But while this development is natural, it isn't automatic. A child will not move from one stage to the next until he or she has been exposed to experiences that allow him or her to practice the skills necessary for making the transition.

Think of it this way: A child may have the muscles and coordination needed to ride a bike but can't actually learn how until one is made available. Similarly, a child must have access to the vehicles of thought in order to capitalize on the maturity of his or her mind.

What does all of this have to do with your child learning to read? Quite a lot, as it turns out. If you want to help your child to become a competent reader, you must provide opportunities for the practice of certain specific skills. The least intrusive way to accomplish this is by exposing your child to books that provide such opportunities while also exhibiting the other characteristics of good books. If the child is ready to assimilate the skills, he or she will; if not, the child will still benefit from everything else the book has to offer.

Nancy Polette regards the concepts of *conservation, classification, seriation,* and *reversibility,* as those portions of Piaget's theories that are relevant to the reading and thinking of young children. She contends that children will not be able to read and think properly until they have mastered these concepts. In *Picture Books for Gifted Programs* she lists many books which help to expose children to them. Most of the titles mentioned below are recommended by her; consult her book for more.

Conservation is the ability to recognize an object even when it changes its shape, its surrounding detail, or its position. Small children who watch juice being poured from a short, fat glass to a tall, skinny one do not recognize that the amount of liquid remains the same because they do not yet have an understanding of conservation. This concept is necessary to reading because a child must recognize the letters of the alphabet in many contexts, sizes, and even colors in order to be able to read.

Books which give practice in conservation include:

The Humbug Witch by Lorna Balian (Nashville, Tennessee: Abingdon Press, 1970)

Mr. Peaknuff's Tiny People by Donna Hill (New York: Atheneum Publishers, 1981)

Whose Cat is That? by Virginia Kahl (New York: Charles Scribner's Sons, 1979)

Classification is the ability to classify objects, characters, and ideas in order to analyze and understand them. Items may be grouped by function; e.g., "things to eat" and "things to wear." High-ability youngsters not only use the common criteria of function, they may also classify by characteristic. Items with lumpy surfaces may be grouped separately from smooth ones regardless of function.

Books which group and regroup objects by color, shape, or size help to introduce this concept. Some examples:

People by Peter Spier (New York: Doubleday, 1980)

Q Is For Duck by Mary Elting and Michael Folsom (New York: Houghton Mifflin, 1980)

Seriation is the ability to place objects, actions, or events in order. Things may be ordered in many ways — for example, by size (increasing or decreasing) or by time. *One Frog Too Many* by Mercer Mayer and Marianna Mayer (New York: Dial Books for Young Readers, 1975) is a story of love, jealousy, and retribution told in pictures only. For your child to appreciate and understand this book, he or she must be able to understand that there is a logical, orderly progression from one action to the next.

Other books that teach seriation include:

Milton the Early Riser by Robert Kraus (New York: Julian Messner, a division of Simon & Schuster, 1981)

Tell Me a Mitzi by Lore Segal (New York, Scholastic, Inc., 1970)

Seriation is equally important to the development of math skills. Books which offer practice in ordering by amount or size include:

Anno's Counting Book by Mitsumaso Anno (New York: Harper & Row, 1975)

Blue Sea by Robert Kalen (New York: Greenwillow Books, 1979)

Reversibility is the ability to trace a line of reasoning back to its beginning. This, too, is important to math as well as reading. A child who has mastered reversibility is one who understands both the literal and the implied meaning of a text. Humor, satire, and poignancy — all staples of good literature — depend on the reader being able to intuitively reverse ideas and roles. Books which aptly introduce this concept include:

A Treeful of Pigs by Arnold Lobel (New York: Greenwillow Books, 1979)

Who's Afraid of the Dark by Bonsall Crosby (New York: Greenwillow Books, 1980)

The Day Jimmy's Boa Ate the Wash by Trinka Nobel (New York: Dial Books for Young Readers, 1980)

□ ■ □

You can make reading even more special by giving your child one or more subscriptions to quality children's magazines. This guarantees that new and interesting material will arrive at your home on a regular basis — and besides, young children love to get mail.

Magazines offer many things books don't: activities, projects, games, puzzles, mazes, cut-outs, and opportunities to draw and color — *verboten* for most books. (Here the no scribble/no dribble rule doesn't have to apply.)

Listed below are magazines of proven interest to young gifted children, loosely ordered from less difficult to more sophisticated. Because gifted children rarely conform to the norms used by publishers to determine audience age, the recommended ages are not given here.

To find out which magazines are right for your child, you may want to write for sample copies before subscribing. Subscription prices noted are current as of March 1986 and are subject to change.

Magazines for Children

Sesame Street Magazine
Children's Television Workshop
200 Watt Street
PO Box 2924
Boulder, CO 80322
Annual subscription price:
$10.95 (6 issues)
Pre-reading, math, and thinking
skills. Projects and games
featuring the Sesame Street
characters.

Your Big Backyard
National Wildlife Federation
1412 16th Street N.W.
Washington, DC 20036
Annual subscription price:
$10.00 (12 issues)
Wildlife and nature study
through stories, games, and
puzzles.

Chickadee
Young Naturalist Foundation
59 Front Street East
Toronto, Ontario M5E 1B3
Canada
Annual subscription price:
$10.95 (10 issues)
Focuses on nature and the
environment; includes features
on other sciences as well as
industry.

Ranger Rick
National Wildlife Federation
1412 16th Street N.W.
Washington, DC 20036
Annual subscription price:
$10.95
A step up in difficulty from *Your
Big Backyard*, but a similar
content of wildlife, natural
history, and environment stories
and activities.

Electric Company Magazine
Children's Television Workshop
200 Watt Street
PO Box 2924
Boulder, CO 80322
Annual subscription price:
$10.95
Games, stories, articles, and
puzzles for Sesame Street
graduates.

Scholastic Let's Find Out
Scholastic Inc.
902 Sylvan Avenue
Englewood Cliffs, NJ 07632
Annual subscription price:
$4.70 (8 issues)
Language arts, social studies,
science and math features. Text
is designed for adults to read to
children (no large print).

**Buddy's Weekly Reader
Publications**
Box 16627
4343 Equity Drive
Columbus, OH 43216
Annual subscription price: $3.90
for 1-9 subscriptions; $1.95 for
10 or more subscriptions (weekly
during the school year)
Science and social studies news
for the beginning reader.

Scholastic News: Pilot 1
Scholastic Inc.
902 Sylvan Ave.
Englewood Cliffs, NJ 07632
Annual subscription price:
$3.40 (26 issues)
Features on places and people
for the beginning reader. *Ranger
2* and *Trails 3*, also available from
Scholastic, are more advanced
versions of the same format.

On Key
JDL Publications
PO Box 1213
Montclair, NJ 07042
Annual subscription price:
$9.00 (6 issues)
Examines the world of music.
Focus on pianists, but of interest
to young musicians in general.

3-2-1 Contact
E²MC Square
200 Watt Street
PO Box 2933
Boulder, CO 80322
Annual subscription price:
$11.95 (10 issues),
$22.95 (20 issues)
Science and technology through
puzzles, projects, and
experiments.

Stone Soup
Children's Art Foundation
PO Box 83
Santa Cruz, CA 95063
Annual subscription price:
$18.00; 2 years, $30.00; 3 years,
$42.00 (bimonthly during the
school year)
Poems, book reviews, and
pictures submitted by children
ages five to twelve.

Cricket
Open Court Publishing
PO Box 2670
Boulder, CO 80322
Annual subscription price:
$17.50
Various styles of writing and
illustrations offer poetry,
folktales, fiction, fantasy, and
nonfiction.

Odyssey
Astro Media Corp.
625 E. St. Paul Avenue
PO Box 92788
Milwaukee, WI 53202
Annual subscription price:
$16.00 (12 issues)
Focus on space and astronomy.

Turtle News
Young People's Logo Association
PO Box 855067
Richardson, TX 75085
Annual subscription price:
$12.00 (12 issues)
Articles, stories, and ideas using
LOGO. For preschool and up.

Current Science
Weekly Reader Publications
Box 16627
4343 Equity Drive
Columbus, OH 43216
Annual subscription price:
$11.00 for 1-9 subscriptions;
$5.50 for 10 or more
subscriptions (biweekly during
the school year)
The latest advances in science
and technology. Designed for
grades six and up, but written
at slightly lower reading levels.
Good readers interested in
science might appreciate the
information but may not relate to
photos and style geared to older
audience.

Cobblestone
Box 959
Farmingdale, NY 11737
Annual subscription price:
$16.50 (12 issues)
Each issue focuses on a theme in
U.S. history.

National Geographic World
17th and M Streets N.W.
Washington, DC 20036
Annual subscription price:
$10.95 (12 issues)
Features wild animals, pets,
hobbies, sports, natural history,
science, and human interest.

Scholastic DynaMath
Scholastic Inc.
902 Sylvan Avenue
Englewood Cliffs, NJ 07632
Annual subscription price: $5.90
(9 issues)
Covers the role of math in the
real world through games,
activities, and a computer page.
A teacher's edition (with
answers) is available.

Zoobooks
Wildlife Education, Ltd.
930 West Washington St.,
San Diego, CA 92103
Annual subscription price:
$14.00 (10 issues)
Each issue features a single
creature — for example, an
eagle. Full-color drawings and
photos throughout, exercises,
detailed but simply written text.

Ahoy
Two Fathoms Publishing
2021 Brunswick Street
Suite 209B
Halifax, Nova Scotia B3K 2Y5
Canada
French language lessons
designed for Canadian children
ages eight and up. Informative
articles, fiction, puzzles, and
reader contributions. Write for
subscription information.

Que'tal? (Spanish)

Das Rad (German)

Bonjour (French)
Scholastic Inc.
902 Sylvan Ave.
Englewood Cliffs, NJ 07632
Annual subscription price:
$5.90 each (8 issues)
Each magazine uses pictures,
stories, word games, and puzzles
to teach the respective language
and culture. Parents should be
aware that although these offer
introductory level instruction
and practice, they are designed
primarily for somewhat older
children.

Recommended Reading

If you want to know more about ways to stimulate and encourage your child to become a reader, try:

The Read-Aloud Handbook by Jim Treleese (New York: Penguin Books, 1982). Tips on how to make the most of the read-aloud experience. Includes hundreds of recommended titles.

Getting Ready to Read by Betty D. Boegehold (New York: Ballantine Books, 1984). Lots of creative and specific ideas.

Sharing Literature with Children by Francelia Butler (New York: David McKay Co., Inc., 1984)

Good Books to Grow On: A Guide to Building Your Child's Library from Birth to Age 5 by Andrea Cascardi (New York: Warner Books, 1985)

Games for Reading: Playful Ways To Help Your Child Read by Peggy Kaye (New York: Pantheon Books, 1984).

Math Activities

A solid math foundation consists of far more than just learning how to count, add, and subtract. A child who is encouraged early to experiment with the concepts basic to an understanding of mathematical principles is developing skills that will be valuable far into the future.

When exposing your child to math-related activities, your primary goal should be to promote a sense of math concepts as powerful tools which can be used in purposeful yet enjoyable ways. Again, drill-and-practice has its place (albeit an insignificant one where young children are concerned), but the majority of math activities should be in the problem-solving realm.

Successful adult mathematicians have three characteristics that set them apart from the rest of us: They have an unusual depth of interest in math concepts; they are ardently enthusiastic about their work in applied mathematics; and they apply an extraordinary amount of effort to it. A parent who encourages the first two characteristics in a child may see the third emerge spontaneously in later years.

In other words, math for children should be *fun*. They should be given math activities they can do, and those activities should mean something to them.

For young children, the best way to ensure mastery of basic math concepts is through manipulatives. Encouraging children to use concrete objects to reach conclusions is consistent with the theories of Piaget — plus kids like it. Playing with a three-dimensional puzzle of an apple, for example, lays the groundwork for the very elementary concept that a whole may be divided into parts. Once grasped, this idea will eventually lead a child to more specific manipulations, from there to fractions, and from there to percentages.

Good math activities are structured to move the young child from the concrete to the abstract. Addition should first be approached through the use of rocks, dried beans, dolls, or raisins, reinforced later with pictures, and finally presented in a purely numerical fashion. Not every math activity requires this progression, but each should incorporate some sort of hands-on experience.

It's fairly easy to make math activities fun. But what about meaningful? Children enjoy applying what they know to solving real-life problems. A child who learns early that math can be useful will be more receptive later on to the months of struggling through the seemingly abstract theory required to master algebra and trigonometry. You help lay the groundwork every time you show your four-year-old how to divide a handful of cookies among a group of friends, collect the right number of utensils for a dinner for five, or count off the days on the calendar until his or her next birthday.

Both concept and computation skills are needed, but when in doubt over which to emphasize, go for concept first. Many parents and educators make the mistake of believing that children should begin with addition, subtraction, multiplication, and division, and only then get into the heavy stuff of theory. In fact, this often creates such profound math anxiety in children that they never choose to advance beyond those functions.

Imagine the ski instructor who teaches children to ski by first having them practice putting on ski equipment. Once they can manage this, the instructor has the children move on to learning to ride the lift, and afterward to stationary drill-and-practice in the configurations required for turning and stopping. Only then are the children allowed to go down an actual hill — provided they haven't yet retired permanently to video games in the chalet. Those few children who do persist may never feel the kind of exhilaration essential to developing a love of skiing.

Beginning mathematicians, like beginning skiers, should be allowed the exhilaration of discovery. Only after they are hooked on that should they be taught the necessary subskills.

These are the math concepts you should explore with your child:

- **Relationships.** How does one item relate to another? To a number of other items? Which is big, bigger, biggest?
- **Spatial concepts.** How do objects function in space? How does a person move through space? What rules govern how objects are put together? (For example, how do LEGOs fit together to form a house, or a boat, or a space station?) What happens to the water line when a glass of liquid is tipped slightly?
- **Categorizing.** What are the attributes of a particular item or group of items? In what ways are these attributes similar? In what ways are they different? Group stones first according to color and then according to size. Figure out how many sets of one plate, one fork, and one spoon will be needed to feed four people. How many of each utensil does this represent?
- **Measurement.** How large, small, tall, wide, heavy is this? How many are there? What time is it? If you go down for your nap in two hours, what time will it be then?
- **Conservation of numbers.** Does the placement of objects affect their total number? Here are seven beans. Put them in a circle. Now put them in a line. Which shape has more beans?
- **Conservation of area and volume.** How does the shape of a container affect how much it will hold? Does a tall container always hold more than a short container? Is a lump of clay "more" when it is formed into a long, skinny snake instead of a ball?
- **Divergent thinking as a solution-finding strategy.** How many different ways might this problem be solved? How many different ways might you group these objects (beans, coins, buttons,

blocks)? How can we figure out when it will be your next birth-day? How can you divide these four cookies between yourself and a friend and both get the same amount? What if you had five cookies?

• **Patterns.** What patterns can you see in a set of objects? How many other ways can you arrange these items to form a pattern?

Are the chairs in the doctor's waiting room different colors? Do these colors always go in the same order, or are they some-times mixed up?

Suggested Home Activities

▼ *Practice spatial relations by working with your child to design inventions.* Examples: a toothbrush for an elephant; a machine to test how balls bounce; an automatic dog walker.

■ *Compare the heights, widths, and lengths of various objects using different units of measure.* How many hands tall is Daddy? How many hands tall are you? How many of your feet wide is the kitchen? How many of Mommy's feet?

● *Give each day a different number, a la Sesame Street: "This day is brought to you by the number_____."* Point out how many times that number is used during the day. "You are four years old. I had to ask you four times to put on your socks. You have four carrots on your plate." Encourage your child to participate in this.

◆ *Make or purchase extra-large dominoes for counting and matching practice.*

▼ *Use cut-up straws for games involving fractions.* Start with a box of plastic straws in assorted colors. Cut all the red ones into fourths, all the green ones in half, all the yellow ones into thirds, etc. Leave some whole.

Then ask your child, "How many red straws does it take to make a line the same length as a white straw? How many to equal a green one? How many to equal two green ones? How many green ones and red ones together make a white one? Can you equal a white one using yellow and green?"

■ *Practice divergent thinking starting with a hand-drawn unicycle, bicycle, and tricycle.* Ask your child to describe how they are different. Then ask, "If we had fifteen wheels, how many unicycles could we have? How many bicycles? How many tricycles? How many combinations?"

Even four- and five-year-olds can handle this if you are willing to sit with them while they laboriously draw the figures. Or save time by cutting out paper "wheels" beforehand and laying them out.

● *Play "store" with real coins.* Keep a money jar handy to fill with loose change. At snack time, "charge" a certain amount for a cookie or a jelly sandwich, and help your child use the change to "pay" for the item.

◆ *Play Bingo to practice number recognition.*

▼ *Practice conservation with a group of similar objects (blocks, buttons, peas, puzzle pieces).* Have your child count the objects. Separate them into two groups and ask, "Do we have the same number now, or a different number?" Encourage your child to begin rearranging the objects himself or herself, each time noting how many are in each group and that the total is the same.

■ *Play "Answer Man" (or "Answer Woman").* Answer Man can only answer questions, not ask them. Start by saying, "The answer is nine." The other player must then think of a question (or questions) which will yield the answer nine. Be sure to let your child play the roles of both questioner and respondent.

● *Help your child develop a sense of time by giving ACCURATE warnings of how much time remains before certain activities will begin or end.* All parents are guilty of telling their children, "Okay, we're going to leave in five minutes," and then dragging it out to ten or twenty or more. Or we toss off comments like, "Pretty soon it will be time for bed." Use a more specific approach: "We will leave for Aunt Sharon's in five minutes," or "In ten minutes it will be time to get ready for bed." Then stick to it!

Get your child involved by providing an easy-to-use egg timer or stopwatch.

◆ *Use "how can you find out" questions to encourage problem-solving.* How can you find out if this table will fit through the door? How can you find out which is bigger, your bunny or your teddy? How can you find out which weighs more, one block or two?

▼ *Set aside an area in the family room or kitchen where the child can keep a supply of manipulatives and other math-related materials.* Examples: sturdy thermometers, scales (two if possible, for comparing weights), current calendars, puzzles with geometric inserts, measuring containers of various sizes (plastic measuring spoons and cups, quart containers, metric measures), sets of beads and strings, blocks, Monopoly money, rulers, a tape measure, buttons, an abacus, a number line, a magnetic board with numbers and letters, etc.

■ *Sort objects into an egg carton or a twelve-cup muffin pan.* Cover two of the 12 sections and label those remaining 0-9. Ask the child to put the correct number of stones, beans, or buttons in each compartment. Help him or her to figure out what happens when an item is moved from one section to another.

● *Use any set of related objects (dolls and plates, horses and blades of grass, children and hats) to introduce the concepts of enough, too many, and too few.* Example: "We have three children and four hats. We have too many _____, and too few _____."

Books That Teach Math Concepts

Anno's Mysterious Multiplying Jar by Masaichiro Anno and Mitsumasa Anno (New York: Putnam Publishing Group, 1983). Recommended for children with a strong talent for math, this book uses Anno's trademark tiny, meticulous drawings to illustrate the nature of factorials — numerical relationships used in figuring probabilities (for example, 3! signifies 3 x 2 x 1, or 6).

3D, 2D, 1D by David Adler (New York: T.Y. Crowell Junior Books, 1975). Introduces the concepts of dimensions.

Number Ideas Through Pictures by Mannis Charosh (New York: T.Y. Crowell Junior Books, 1974).

Number Families by Jane Jonas Srivastava (New York: T.Y. Crowell Junior Books, 1979).

— Creative Publications offers problem-solving materials based on math but with strong visual components. Puzzle posters include visual challenges (example: solve a ratio based on columns of multicolored concentric circles), math activities, mazes. Other posters are based on mathematical design themes (examples: stained-glass tessellations, the geometry of patchwork quilts, patterns in honeycombs, spiderwebs, snowflakes, seashells). Most are accompanied by explanatory booklets. Also available: materials for designing one's own games — blank boards, spinners, blank cards, cubical or polyhedral dice.

Request a free catalog by writing: Creative Publications, PO Box 10328, Palo Alto, CA 94303.

— DUPLO Mosaic Sets from LEGO Systems, Inc. teach children to identify colors and shapes, and to create patterns and designs. Sets include idea cards and colored pieces that interlock with the DUPLO building plate. Available by mail order only; write: LEGO Systems, Inc., Susan Williams, PO Box 938, Enfield, CT 06082.

Science Activities

Successful practicing scientists share many characteristics, the most notable among them being curiosity — constant, unending curiosity. The parent who capitalizes on a child's natural curiosity lays the foundation for further science education.

To promote curiosity among young scientists, it helps to regard science study as a process rather than a discrete body of knowledge. We should let our children's questions guide us to a subject of study, and then let the process dictate how we approach this study. We won't lack for possibilities; it's estimated that the average four-year-old asks nearly 300 questions every day!

A streamlined version of the scientific process goes like this:

1. Start by observing a particular phenomenon.

2. Ask questions about why it is the way it is or how it might be changed.

3. Hypothesize answers to your own questions.

4. Gather information that will help to prove (or disprove) your hypotheses, and record your results.

5. Generalize what you have learned, and perhaps apply it to other situations.

This may sound too complicated for young children, but it really isn't. Consider, for example, a typical child's question: "Why does a stick float and a rock sink?" The first and second steps of the process have already been accomplished: A phenomenon has been observed, and a question has been asked. The third step is to make some guesses about the phenomenon. With a little subtle guidance, your child should be able to come up with some that include references to weight, substance, shape, etc. The fourth step is to gather information. Collect items that conform to the variables of weight, substance, shape, etc. that you have hypothesized, then drop them one by one into a lake or a bucket of water. Note which float and which do not. Ask still more questions: Are there similarities among the items that float? Among those that don't? Are there differences among them? Consult any other available sources, such as books or articles, and discuss how the data you have gathered fits with what you have read. End with the fifth step — making some generalizations and collecting a new batch of items, this time trying to predict which will float.

Not too hard, yet consistent with the procedures used by scientific researchers. And, of course, not every science experiment must include every component of this process.

Much of the seemingly random play common to young children contains elements of scientific inquiry. If your child went through the typical toddler stage of stuffing anything and everything into the toilet, he or she made a number of observations (soap floats; trucks sink; teddy bears float, get soggy, sink slowly, and get stuck). Then he or she probably went on to draw up a hypothesis (soap likes to be on top of water, trucks like to be under water, teddy bears don't like to be anywhere in water). Even though the hypothesis wasn't necessarily "correct," the process was still sound. Given the opportunity, a child will keep practicing these steps until he or she reaches a correct hypothesis. It may take months or even years, but that, too, is part of what it's all about.

If this approach seems overly structured to you, you may want to borrow an idea from Ulysses Weldon.* He suggests that parents consider the "three T's" as well as the three R's — the three

---

* Ulysses Weldon, "Teach the Three T's," *Gifted Children Monthly* (December 1985), p. 15.

T's being *talking, tinkering,* and *traveling.* For example, if your child wants to know where the sun goes at night, start by talking about his or her observations and some possible answers. Then tinker around with a flashlight and balls of various sizes to simulate the rotation of the earth. Finally, travel together to a place where you can clearly view a sunrise or a sunset. Simple, but effective.

Good science activities address children's questions in a way that enhances their curiosity while directing them toward specific behaviors. They focus on these concepts:

• **Comparing and contrasting.** How is this item like that one? How are they different?

• **Classifying.** Is this item enough like that one that we could put them in the same group? What kind of a group is this?

• **Predicting.** What will happen if...?

• **Observing.** What does an object look like? What color and shape is it? How does it feel, smell, sound, taste?

• **Relating cause and effect.** What will happen if we do this? What do you think caused this to happen? How might we cause this to happen? How might we prevent this from happening?

Suggested Home Activities

 Invest in small but real screwdrivers and hammers and let your child take apart old appliances and other junk items. Start with non-electrical items (old alarm clocks, tricycles, flashlights). If your budding mechanic insists on moving on to toasters and the like, start every project by *removing the cord* so it's impossible to plug in.

It's not necessary that the items be put back together again; just letting the child examine their workings is sufficient at this point.

 Keep a child-sized knapsack packed for expeditions. Standard equipment should include a magnifying glass for botanical, zoological, and geological studies; a jar with an aerated lid to house critters; a large, sturdy spoon for digging; assorted paper cups, margarine tubs, and other containers for storing treasures; and a small first-aid kit.

Tape-record a sound collection, then compare sounds from different locations. Or play the tape for someone else and have him or her guess the sources of the sounds.

Mount a thermometer with large numbers where your child can see it easily. This can be the focal point for various activities. For example, set some guidelines for what types of clothing should be worn at what temperatures, and let your child dress himself or herself after first checking the thermometer. Or have your child keep track of the temperature hour-by-hour throughout the day, then make predictions about the next day.

Have your child observe the weather and record his or her observations. Make or purchase stickers representing the different kinds of weather (sunny, stormy, snowy, rainy, hot, cold, windy, etc.) Check the weather together every morning and evening and have your child put the appropriate stickers on the calendar.

Make a "body shirt." Have your child use fabric crayons to make a t-shirt depicting some of his or her internal organs — heart, lungs, kidneys. Your local library should have one or more anatomy books written for children; use these as sources of information and simple illustrations to copy or trace. For less coordinated little hands, you may wish to outline the organs and let the child decorate and color them. Kids love wearing their innards on their outards.

Introduce the concepts of permanence and change by making lists to consult while driving or waiting. Ask your child, "What are all the things about yourself that you could change? What are all the things that have to stay the same?" Vary the game by making lists for other family members, pets, and inanimate objects.

Use a magnifying glass to explore hair, skin, fingernails, etc. Compare the "looks" of different individuals. Compare human hair and nails to those of the family pet.

Play "Who Belongs to the Club?" Start by listing several items having similar characteristics, such as types of fruit. Explain that bananas, apples, and oranges all belong to this "club." Then ask, "Does a ball of dirt belong to this club? An onion? A grape?"

Use cooking activities to demonstrate that properties change when subjected to mixing, heat, etc. Focus on before-and-after comparisons: "What color was the batter before the eggs were added? After? What utensils did we move to use the cookies around before they were baked? After?"

Make a "cookbook" from pictures of foods cut from magazines. Help your child to arrange them on the pages according to how they are prepared — for example, one page for boiled foods, another for baked, another for peeled, etc. Don't worry if some confusion results over foods requiring more than one type of preparation; it's important for your child to grasp the concept that an item can have more than one variable to compare.

Take a "smelly walk." Talk with your child about all of the different things he or she can smell. Classify the smells as animal, vegetable, or mechanical in origin.

Keep a growth book for a particular tree or bush. Either plant one with your child to call his or her own, or adopt an already maturing one. Note in the growth book any changes in foliage, measurements, water requirements, etc.

Make a sand table. Sand tables are popular in British kindergartens because they provide endless play opportunities. Fill a large cake pan or baking pan with cornmeal, oatmeal, sand, or dried beans. Then let your child play in it with spoons, measuring cups, little cars and people, whatever.

Prepare a series of "nose ticklers." Put small amounts of familiar-smelling substances (peanut butter, white paste, cinnamon) in small paper cups and cover them with tinfoil or a paper towel secured by a rubber band. Poke a small hole in the covers and see whether your child can identify the contents by smell. Help him or her to label the types of smells (sweet, sharp, strong, gentle, spicy, etc.). Ask, "What kinds of pictures does this smell make in your mind? What do you think of when you smell that smell? How does it make you feel?"

Play "Simon Says" using attributes for comparison. Examples: "Simon Says step on the rough area of the ground." "Simon Says run to a tree that is fatter than that elm tree."

Have your child describe how things look from different viewpoints. "What does a tree look like if you lie under it... if you stand very close to it... if you stand across the yard from it?"

Give your child a magnet and several small objects (pins, buttons, dice, beans, coins, etc.). Have your child separate the objects into two piles — those he or she thinks a magnet will pick up, and those he or she thinks it won't. Experiment to confirm or disprove this hypothesis.

— Edmund Scientific offers several kits for science-minded tinkerers, as well as lenses, prisms, magnets, solar cells, and tools. It also has one of the best beginner's telescopes on the market, the Astroscan 2001. The Astroscan looks strange (like a bright red upside-down lightbulb) but sets up in seconds to give a clear, bright, wide-angle view of the heavens. It's not cheap, but if you're in the market for a family telescope you may want to consider it. For a free catalog of kits and science apparatus, or for more information on the Astroscan, write: Edmund Scientific, 101 E. Gloucester Pike, Barrington, NJ 08007.

— Learning Things has science apparatus as well as playful things — frames for making cubic and prismic bubbles, rhombic construction puzzles, and coiled-wire puzzles; a microscope/projector, tools, and supplies for cardboard carpentry; and a finely balanced gyroscope. For a free catalog, write: Learning Things, Inc., PO Box 436, Arlington, MA 02174.

Creativity Activities

Even more than the other activities described in this chapter, those aimed at stimulating creativity must be viewed in context. Unlike language, math, and science, creativity cannot be separated from other forms of human learning and endeavor. Regardless of the subject matter, any innovative or important work in a field occurs because an individual has applied techniques of creative problem-solving in combination with his or her expertise. While it's possible to be creative in isolation from any specific discipline, the converse is not true.

There's a standard piece of folk wisdom that *all* young children are highly creative. Like other widely-held beliefs, this is based both on misunderstandings and on grains of truth.

Definitions formulated by researchers in the field suggest that creativity is an intellectual and emotional activity that occurs when an individual uses discipline and effort to break away from typical patterns of thought. Though whimsical and endearing, many behaviors of young children do not meet these criteria. Adults tend to perceive these behaviors as creative because they do indeed appear to break away from typical thought patterns; what we fail to realize, however, is that they are fairly commonplace among children. More important, they're not the result of *applying* expertise, but of *insufficient* expertise. And often they are totally inadvertent. (Children do all sorts of things by accident that it would take adults a great deal of time and effort to accomplish.)

When Picasso painted a woman with three faces, he was breaking away from established practice to express his own unique ideas about the nature of women and of human beings. When a child paints a chicken with three eyes, it is not so much an innovation in barnyard art as it is an indication of the child's lack of observation and artistic skills.

Now for the grains of truth in the folk wisdom. Children are, in fact, problem-solvers in ways that are even more impressive and sophisticated than the superficial creativity of three-eyed chickens. They are creative and innovative in ways that are consistent with longstanding theories of creativity. Their efforts reflect determination as well as imagination.

During the 1920s, Graham Wallas identified four stages of the creative process:

1. Preparation, which involves study, research, and experimentation;

2. Incubation, which occurs when the conscious mind relaxes and focuses on some other activity than the problem at hand;

3. Illumination, in which a solution appears to spontaneously "jump" from the unconscious to the conscious; and

4. Verification, in which the results of the problem-solving effort are checked for accuracy and the original idea is elaborated on.

Watch any baby and you will see this process dozens of times a day. Consider little Jennifer splashing in her bath. Although she isn't making the connection between her flailing limbs and the flying water, she is nevertheless experiencing the preparation (or experimentation) stage of problem-solving, the problem being one of how to repeat the pleasurable effect of splashing. Following a pause in the action, Mom might begin a shampoo or a soothing rubdown with a washcloth. During this time the baby is no longer concerned with splashing, but with the other sensory experiences now underway. This is the incubation phase, and a different part of her mind is busy tackling the problem.

When Jennifer starts moving around again, it's almost as if a lightbulb blinks on over her head. An arm is accidentally slapped against the surface of the water...the connection is made between action and reaction...and splashing begins with a vengeance! This is the final verification stage of the process, in which the baby checks again and again to see that the solution (which seemed to occur as a bolt out of the blue) is correct. If the bath lasts long enough, she may even begin to elaborate on her original discovery and try to get a similar effect with different limbs or a clutched object.

So all we parents really need to do to encourage creativity in our children is to help them maintain the capacity for problem-solving they were born with. This is both easy and hard to do —

easy in that we don't have to develop or participate in any elaborate schemes, hard in that our society seems at times to conspire
against individuality and innovation.

We can use both *passive* and *active* strategies to promote creativity. The passive strategies have to do with how we respond to
certain behaviors in our children. The active strategies are fun
and playful techniques which provide children with the sort of
mental exercise that helps them to approach problems creatively.

Passive strategies tend to be don'ts rather than do's. Some
recommendations:

Avoid squashing experimentation and idea formation. As
parents, we must be careful not to imply that everything our children do must end in success, that they are not to diverge from the
norm, and that they must always be "making good use of their
time." Remember that incubation is critical to problem-solving.
Children who are gainfully employed every minute never have the
chance to daydream, doodle, and be frivolous — activities during
which incubation occurs.

Avoid killer phrases that inhibit your child. You know the
ones: "That's impossible," "Somebody has already done that,"
"That's very nice, dear, but it would be even better if you...," "Be
careful or you'll make a mistake." And the worst of all: "I told
you so!"

Instead, we should encourage our children to judge for themselves the worth of a particular product or solution; request
unique and original work ("Do you think you could draw for me an
animal that no one else has ever seen?"); and reward imaginative
thought with admiration and praise.

Active strategies do not necessarily yield practical products,
but instead are designed to allow for the development of techniques that might come in handy later. Some suggestions:

Brainstorming. Even small children can practice brainstorming. The rules are simple: Everyone tries to generate as many
ideas as possible, any answer is acceptable, and no one is allowed
to criticize anyone else's ideas.

The more ideas, the more successful the brainstorming session. A breakfast game of "What should we do today?" is one that any child who can talk is capable of handling.

Forced relationships. Children are encouraged to play with ideas about what would happen if two dissimilar objects or situations were juxtaposed or combined. For example: "What could we make if we used the parts of your teddy bear and the parts of your Gobot?" (The clock-radio and the wheelchair resulted from this type of thinking.)

Guided fantasy. Start by helping your child to relax through massage and deep-breathing techniques. Then say, "Close your eyes and try to imagine pictures that go with what I'm about to say." Guide your child through a balloon ride over your block, a trip down a wild river, or an excursion into the jungle. Give minimal descriptions and ask the child to fill in the details. "Now we are flying over Randy's house.... Look down from our balloon and see what is happening in his yard...."

Activities like these give your child the sense that creative endeavor is meaningful and worthwhile. They reinforce the notion that innovation is a positive approach to problem-solving and allow your child to begin developing what John Gowan, a noted researcher and educator of the gifted, suggests are the two main forms of creativity: *personal* creativity and *cultural* creativity.

Personal creativity occurs when one solves a problem for himself or herself. For a solution to be deemed personally creative, one must think up an idea that is new to him or her, or elaborate on a known idea in some unique way. Cultural creativity occurs when one creates a solution to a problem that affects many people, and the solution is accepted by the general population of a particular culture. Many gifted individuals achieve various forms of cultural creativity (Thomas Alva Edison, Buckminster Fuller).

When looking for activities that will encourage creativity in your child, remember that creative endeavor is not some magical end product of daydreaming and flightiness. It takes trial and error and lots of hard work. Educator, author, and noted researcher in creativity E. Paul Torrance compares it to the Japanese concept of *sartori,* a degree of expertness in which sudden flashes of insight occur as a result of intense devotion, constant and sustained practice, self-discipline, and expended energy.* The child in hot pursuit of something that interests him or her may be considered headed toward this ideal state. It's up to us as parents to get out of the way!

Suggested Home Activities

Organize outings in response to specific questions. Going to the dump may not be your idea of a good time, but the four-year-old who wonders what happens to the garbage when it leaves the can may find it thrilling.

Show respect for your child's artwork. Hang it in places of honor and save it in folders. Interviews with established artists indicate that some of their earliest and most encouraging memories involved parents who openly cherished their work.

Provide a variety of artistic media for your child to work with. Break out of the paper-and-pencil routine. Fingerpaint with pudding or soft jello; make collages out of wallpaper scraps, different fabrics, strings, buttons, and the like; make your own playdough (see page 120).

When reading aloud, stop before the end of the story and ask, "And then what happened?" Give as much credence to the made-up version as to the "real" ending.

Another technique that makes reading interesting is to end each session at a cliff-hanging moment — and keep the child wondering and imagining what's to come.

Play fanciful games in the car by asking "How do you think those clouds got there?" "Where do pineapples come from?" The sillier the answer, the better.

Tell piggyback stories. Each person starts a simple story and stops at a crucial point. The next person picks up where he or she left off, and so on. Keep the adult parts short and simple.

Make a game out of thinking up ways to replace or improve ordinary household objects. Try, "What if we were stranded on the moon and didn't have a toothbrush? What could we use to

---

* E. Paul Torrance, *Search for Sartori & Creativity* (Buffalo, New York: Creative Education Foundation, Inc., 1979).

clean our teeth?" Go for lots of answers. Or, "This bed is hard to make. How could we change it so it would be easier?" (The person who invented Velcro had to start somewhere.)

Have your child take on the identity of a household object. Model the behavior you're looking for by pretending something like this: "Ooh, I really like being a blender. I get to crunch and munch and bunch everybody's lunch. It's fun when a malt slooshes around all cool and creamy on my insides. But I don't like grinding carrots; that hurts!" As your child starts developing his or her own "character," be ready with questions: "Where do you live? What do you like most about your job?"

Keep an "analogy jar." Each family member writes the names of objects, animals, plants, whatever on individual slips of paper and puts them in the jar. Then each player draws two slips of paper and tries to think of ways in which the objects named are alike. ("How is an owl like a radio?" "How is a refrigerator like a book?" "How is Uncle Fred like a telephone?")

Make lists of all the things you can do with a shoe. A hairbrush. A set of measuring cups.

Keep a tape recorder running as your child works on various art or language projects. Later your child will enjoy listening and remembering the steps he or she used in the creative process.

Ask comparison questions that stimulate the imagination. Which is heavier, a smile or a frown? Which is sharper, fear or anger? Which is rounder, peanut butter or rocks? Which is faster, the wind or a car? (Note: Young children either love this or hate it. Those who are still literal-minded find it confusing and annoying. Don't push the child who refuses to play.)

□ ■ □

Creative adults often speak of "falling in love" with a particular subject or idea as a child. This love affair later turns into a successful and useful career. These early years are a time to explore many different topics and skills so that your child may eventually find something with which to fall in love.

Books That Promote Creativity

Andrew Henry's Meadow by Doris Burn (New York: Putnam Publishing Group, 1965). Andrew Henry, the undervalued inventor, joins neighborhood children in building a magical world.

And To Think That I Saw it On Mulberry Street by Dr. Seuss (New York: Vanguard Press, 1937). In this vintage Seuss, young Marco practices the creative techniques of coming up with many ideas and elaborating on each.

Daydreamers by Tom Feelings and Eloise Greenfield (New York: Dial Books for Young Readers, 1981). Describes a world of fantasy and daydreams.

The Gorilla Did It by Barbara Hazen (New York: Atheneum Publishers, 1974). An imaginary playmate gets blamed for problems.

Round Trip by Ann Jonas (New York: Greenwillow Books, 1983). A family trip is illustrated from front to back of this book, while the return trip (the same pictures upside-down) reads from back to front.

Topsy-Turvies: Pictures to Stretch the Imagination by Mitsumasa Anno (New York: John Weatherhill Inc., 1970). Odd perspectives allow illustrations to be viewed from opposite directions. Follow up with *Upside-Downers: More Pictures to Stretch the Imagination* from the same author and publisher (1971).

The Maggie B. by Irene Hass (New York: Atheneum Publishers, 1975). A young girl's wish comes true when she and her baby brother sail on a fantasy boat.

Virtually anything by Chris Van Allsburg, whose stories are known for their fascinating, dreamlike twists and detailed illustrations of amazing occurrences.

Art Activities

A primary reason for involving young children in art activities* is to help them start developing a sound aesthetic sense. Personal taste is necessary for one to become either a consumer or a producer of art. To acquire an aesthetic sense, a child must master some fundamental concepts and skills, including:

• **The understanding that art is a way to create images.** A drawing, a dance, and a performance are all images that symbolize things, ideas, or emotions. Given the opportunity, even preschool children can discover that certain color combinations make them feel certain emotions, or that different types of music can make them want to move in different ways.

• **The ability to make basic judgments regarding art.** From the very beginning, children can learn to recognize that one sound is stronger than another, or that drawing this picture is more pleasurable than drawing that one. Through careful questioning, you can even help your child to determine which components of a work of art led him or her to arrive at a particular judgment about it.

For example, if a specific piece of music makes a child feel "jumpy," he or she can probably determine why — because of the sound of the notes, their pattern, the speed at which they were played, the rhythm, or some combination of these.

• **The ability to perceive art as both a pleasurable and a personal experience.** Especially at this age, developing an aesthetic sense does not mean being able to recognize certain paintings, artists, or schools of expression. Instead, it means recognizing that profound and delightful thoughts and ideas may be represented by a number of physical or auditory means.

□ ■ □

Visual literacy actually occurs *before* other forms of communication mastery. In other words, it is not so much that we must teach

---

* For purposes of this discussion, art activities will be taken to mean the visual arts (painting, drawing, and sculpting) as well as the performing arts (music, dance, and theater). Certain types of writing, while also art forms, are covered in the "Language Activities" section, pages 68-76.

our children to be visually astute, but rather that we should encourage them to use and improve a skill they already have.

Infants have a fairly large visual "vocabulary" which is initially passive but rapidly becomes active. Even before they bestow their first smile, they respond to facial expressions, gestures, and movements on the part of caregivers, and it is not long until they are sending out messages themselves. Anyone who has ever left an unwilling toddler with a babysitter knows that a child doesn't need words — a quivering lip, droopy shoulders, and agony-filled eyes are sufficient to get the point across.

This early sensitivity to visual stimuli needs to be nurtured into a learned appreciation of art forms. This is especially relevant in our society, where children are bombarded from birth with mass-media concepts of visual communication. Much of the billboard or TV art that is shoved at children is crude, pretentious, bland, or trite; a steady diet can twist sensitivity into a taste for mediocrity.

Quality art experiences can provide an antidote to these inappropriate stimuli and help children to become enlightened consumers of both pop culture and fine art. Activities that nurture early visual literacy have the following characteristics:

• They encourage children to "speak" visually about things that are important to them or of interest to them.
• They encourage children to use and trust their own judgment regarding art.
• They clarify and affirm children's feelings and perceptions.
• They encourage purposeful art experiences that allow children to communicate with meaningful audiences.
• They allow in-depth experimentation with varied media.
• They whet the child's appetite for further artistic expression.

Suggested Visual Art Home Activities

Provide your child with as many opportunities as possible to use different art media — watercolors, tempera paints, clay, wood, paper, etc.

Whenever your child creates an original work, take the time to respond. Start by asking the child to describe the techniques he or she used. For example: "How did you get the sun to be both orange and yellow at the same time?" "How many colors did it take to make that house?" "How did you get the warts to stick on the monster?"

Comment on specific areas of success. For example: "I see you used all the primary colors." "You did a whole painting in shades of red." "The squirrel is the brightest thing in your picture. It really stands out...." "Your sculpture shape has jutting-out places on each side. That means it has balance."

Save various works and bring them together at a later date to compare them. Ask, "Do you like any of these better than the others? Why? Was one more interesting to paint than another? Which uses the most colors? The fewest? How did you feel when you painted this? How do you feel when you look at it now?" Or, "Here is a painting of a truck and the model you made out of a box. How are they alike? How are they different?"

Save boxes of all sizes (the bigger, the better) to use as cardboard sculpture materials. Encourage your child to decorate his or her sculptures and structures.

Keep an "art box" on hand. Fill it with new and unusual items, not just paint, paper, and clay. Consider feathers, buttons, fabric scraps, oatmeal, colored sand, shape stickers, styrofoam, etc.

Use felt pieces of different colors and sizes to make pictures or shapes on a flannel board.

Cut tints and shades of the same color out of construction paper or fabric and ask your child to put them in order from light to dark.

To sharpen your child's observation skills, offer a tray of objects and ask your child to look at them for one minute. Then remove the tray and ask your child to describe as many objects as he or she can remember.

Make a lotto or concentration game using cut-up prints of famous paintings. You can find inexpensive prints in some art supply stores and at museum shops.

Encourage careful observation on a trip to the museum (or using reprints). Ask specific questions like, "Are there any triangles in this picture? Where? How many? What colors are used? How does this picture make you feel? Tell me a story about what is happening in this picture."

Cut sponges into different shapes, dip in tempera paint, and print patterns on large sheets of paper.

Work with your child on a "magic" painting. Have your child draw with crayon on a sheet of paper and then wash over it with thinned paint (an interesting effect!).

Spend a rainy afternoon making playdough. You'll need 1 cup of flour, 1/3 cup of salt, a few drops of vegetable oil, and enough water to make 1/3 to 1/2 cup of dough. Mix and color with food coloring or tempera paint (the colors will be more vivid than in the purchased product). Store in an airtight plastic bag.

□ ■ □

Music, dance, and theater require not only that a piece be created but that it also be performed. The performer may be the originator of the work or someone else. In any event, the performer must master specific skills before going in front of an audience.

One can begin producing visual art at almost the same time one begins consuming it, but the usual progression in the performing arts is *first* to consume the work of others, *second* to learn to perform the work of others, and *finally* (if ever) to create one's own work. It is possible to achieve a great deal of recognition and respect as a musician or a dancer without ever composing a phrase or choreographing a movement.

These differences have led to widely varying approaches in the teaching of the visual arts and the performing arts. Educators in the former field tend to advocate giving children considerable freedom to "mess around" with a range of media, working up gradually to specific techniques and formal instruction. In contrast, three-year-olds are routinely introduced to specific skills on the violin or steps in the dance. There are distinct schools of thought regarding the proper way to proceed with formal educa-

tion and the proper age at which to begin it. The bottom line is
that your child can begin instruction in music or dance at a very
early age, should you choose to have him or her participate.

It is not within the scope of this book to describe criteria for
evaluating early exposure in these areas. Even the experts dis-
agree, for example, on the best age to start music lessons. Some
say to wait until age seven or eight, when the child is old enough
to accept the discipline required for serious study of any kind.
Others say to start as soon as the child can hold a scaled-down
Suzuki violin.

What's best for *your* child? Keep these questions in mind
when considering music lessons:

- Who really wants the lessons, you or your child?
- Are reading and counting necessary for success? If so, are
your child's skills up to the task?
- How good is your child's ear? (A tone-deaf child will have a
hard time playing the violin). How is his or her finger coordination?
- Can your child sit still for a solid half-hour? Will he or she last
out a lesson or tolerate having to practice?
- Will the child be able to practice often and regularly? Or will
practice conflict with other interests? Or is your home life too
unstructured to allow for such a commitment?

It goes without saying that a young child who really doesn't
want to take lessons shouldn't be forced to take lessons. This can
led to a lifelong avoidance and even dislike of music, a terrible
price to pay.

What about choosing a teacher? This is something you will want to do very carefully, since the teacher your child ends up with will profoundly influence how he or she feels about music both now and in the future. (Fortunately, the knuckle-rapping piano teacher seems a thing of the past.) Use these questions as a starting point:

• Is the teacher enthusiastic about music? Enthusiasm is as important as musical skill or experience.
• Does the teacher enjoy working with children?
• How does the teacher reward and discipline young students?
• How much will the teacher expect you to become involved? How involved are you willing to get?
• What instructional philosophy does the teacher follow?

Consider alternatives to private lessons. There are preschool music programs that include such activities as eurhythmics (body movements used to teach musical concepts) and group ensembles in which bells, drums, and other instruments provide enjoyable social experiences while teaching basic skills. Here again, instructional philosophies vary from the relaxed to the highly structured.

The *National Guild of Community Schools of the Arts Membership Directory* lists over 120 schools of the performing arts. See if your local library has a copy, or write: National Guild of Community Schools of the Arts, PO Box 583 West Englewood Station, Teaneck, NJ 07666.

The *Informed Performer's Directory of Instruction for the Performing Arts* by Kat Smith (New York: Avon Books, 1985) is a guide to classes and coaches all over the nation.

The MacPhail Center for the Arts in Minneapolis (an extension of the University of Minnesota) has considerable experience teaching children starting as young as two and a half. They recommend that music classes allow children to:

• listen to, move to, and act out what they hear;
• explore simple concepts such as rhythm, texture, and form by participation;

- respond to melody, rhythm, and timbre;
- experience patterns of sound and rhythm;
- have access to many forms of active noise and music making;
- combine movement, language, and singing;
- focus on aesthetic perception and awareness; and
- create, with adult guidance, their own simple musical forms.

According to the MacPhail Center, dance classes should offer opportunities to:

- respond physically to music;
- design shapes with the body and with other bodies;
- move alone and as a group;
- develop ease of movement;
- become comfortable with the limits and abilities of the body;
- learn how one's body functions in space;
- practice exercises in body placement;
- improve one's strength, flexibility, coordination, and balance; and
- practice expressiveness using the body.

Only you can be the judge of whether a particular teacher, school, program, or approach is working for your child. At this stage, what's most important is for your child to genuinely enjoy *any* art experience. He or she should derive real pleasure from seeing or making a painting, hearing or making music, watching or doing a dance. Ideally, your child will learn to communicate through voice, instruments, *and* body movements, not just one or the other of these. Early experiences should be varied and sensory in nature, affirming again the child's perceptions of the world.

The following activities are intended to promote awareness of the performing arts without conflicting with any instructional philosophy you may later choose for your child.

Suggested Music and Movement Home Activities

♪ *Have your child memorize short poems that have a regular beat, chant them, and march to them. An example: "Engine, Engine, Number Nine/Going down Chicago Line/If that train goes off* the track/Will I get my money back?" Start slow and repeat faster and faster, and this will take on the sound of a train speeding up.

♪ *Encourage your child to respond to music in a wide variety of ways.* Try: "Pretend you're a snake (elephant, cat, bird). Now, how would you move to this music?" "Have different parts of your body (just your head, just your fingers, just your eyebrows) dance to the beat." "Try walking (clapping, galloping, slithering, melting, shaking, rattling, tumbling, skipping, spinning) in time to the music." "Move quietly (lightly, heavily, slowly, quickly, strongly). Move as if you're happy (afraid, angry, silly, tired)."

♪ *Put together an "orchestra" of homemade instruments.* Some suggestions:

♪ Fill containers (plastic margarine tubs, empty oatmeal boxes) with different substances (beads, sand, oatmeal, marbles, buttons) to make shakers. Have your child use them to imitate different sounds (leaves rustling, wind blowing, feet scuffling).

♪ Cover blocks with sandpaper to make rhythm blocks. Have your child imitate the sounds of carpenters sanding, squirrels running through leaves, snakes slithering, ladies dancing in long dresses, a heavy wind.

♪ Hammer nails into a board at different intervals and stretch rubber bands of different thicknesses across them for a homemade plucking and strumming instrument. Have your child imitate the sounds of rain falling, people stretching, cats yowling, a giant laughing.

♪ Let your child use pan lids as cymbals to imitate thunder, the garbage truck, stomping feet. (In most houses this exercise isn't allowed to go on too long, but it's fun while it lasts.)

♪ Make rhythm sticks from two plain dowel rods. If possible, have a woodworker groove half of each one on a lathe so they can be rubbed together as rough and smooth. Have your child imitate woodpeckers, hoofbeats, running feet, the sounds of teeth being brushed.

♪ Make drums from ice-cream pails, coffee cans, etc. Have your child imitate a far-off storm, a close-by storm, anger, a marching band, stomping feet, tiptoeing feet.

♪ Fill glasses with differing amounts of water and let your child play them with a spoon.

Bear, koala, and penguin tambourines, frog and monkey handbells, frog maracas, a myna bird whistle, and duck, clown, panda, and frog castanets are available through JTG of Nashville, 1024C 18th Avenue South, Nashville, TN 37212. All are made of rugged, colorful molded plastic. Write or call 1-800-222-2584 (in Tennessee, call 615/329-3036).

□ ■ □

The best way to help your child develop an appreciation for music is by making it a regular part of your home life. Play it while preparing meals, while your child is working on art projects, while straightening up the house. Play calming music before nap or bedtime, rousing music in the morning, and a variety in between.

There's also a lot of quality children's music available today. The artists are authentic musicians who sing and play to children without patronizing them. An added advantage is that many parents find that they can listen to these albums or tapes over and over without going crazy.

Your local public library should have a selection of the following. Or check with a quality toy store. Order information is provided in the event your searches prove unsuccessful.

Recommended Recordings for Children

For the very young:

Music for 1's and 2's, sung and played by Tom Glazer. For ordering information, write: CMS Records, Inc., 14 Warren Street, New York, NY 10007.

For late two and up:

Baby Beluga, Rise and Shine, Singable Songs, More Singable Songs, Raffi's Christmas Album, and *The Corner Grocery Store* by Raffi. Write: Troubador Records Ltd., 6043 Yonge Street, Willowdale, Ontario, Canada M2M 3W3.

One Elephant, Deux Elephants, Elephant Jam, Smorgasbord, and *Singing 'n Swinging* by Sharon, Lois and Bram. Write: Elephant Records, P.O. Box 101, Station Z, Tor, Canada M4M 2Z3.

I Know The Colors of the Rainbow and *One and Two, Jambo* by Ella Jenkins. Write: Folkways & Scholastic Records, 632 Broadway, New York, NY 10012.

Other artists and titles to try:

Pete Seeger, *Abiyoyo, American Folk Songs for Children, Birds, Beasts, Bugs and Bigger Fishes.* Write: Folkways & Scholastic Records, 632 Broadway, New York, NY 10012.

Fred Penner, *The Cat Came Back, The Polka Dot Pony,* and *Special Delivery.* Write: Shoreline Records, c/o RCA Victor, 1133 Avenue of the Americas, New York, NY 10036.

Books that Stimulate Interest in the Arts

Any good children's picture book is an exercise in art appreciation. The following also deal directly with the subject of art:

Frederick by Leo Lionni (New York: Pantheon Books, 1966). While other animals gather food for the winter, Frederick gathers colors and stories to sustain the family's hearts and souls.

Oliver Button Is a Sissy by Tomie dePaola (New York: Harcourt Brace Jovanovich, Inc., 1979). Oliver pursues his love of dance and performing even in the face of taunts.

Anno's Journey by Mitsumasa Anno (New York: Putnam Publishing Group, 1978). Anno travels through the art and architecture of Europe.

Ben's Trumpet by Rachel Isadora (New York: Greenwillow Books, 1979). Young Ben wants to be a jazz musician but doesn't have a trumpet. Fine illustrations in art deco style.

No Good in Art by Miriam Cohen and Lillian Hoban (New York: Greenwillow Books, 1980). A creative child has both diminishing and enriching experiences in art class.

A Very Young Dancer by Jill Krementz (New York: Alfred A. Knopf, Inc., 1976). A young dancer's life, in words and photographs.

Talking to the Sun: An Illustrated Anthology of Poetry for Young People by Kenneth Koch and Kate Farrell (New York: Holt, Rinehart & Winston, 1985). A selection of poems, illustrated with works from the Metropolitan Museum of Art.

Finally, don't feel compelled to stick with children's books alone. Art is an area in which adult "picture books" may also appeal to children. One in particular was a big hit with a six-year-old we know: *Metropolitan Cats* by John P. O'Neill (New York: The Metropolitan Museum of Art/Harry N. Abrams, 1981), which features paintings of cats (or with cats somewhere in them) from the Museum's collection.

CHAPTER 6

Toys: Tools for the Work of Children

Play is the work of children; toys are the tools children use to develop myriad skills and abilities. They may be as simple as a stick found on a walk, or as elaborate as a computerized baby doll and accessories. In either case, the play generated by a particular toy has the potential to provide valuable benefits to your child.

Children at play...

...learn to control their bodies and develop physical strength,

...express their feelings,

...develop sensory awareness,

...practice problem-solving by figuring out how things work,

...learn alternative ways to communicate,

...develop imagination and creativity, and

...practice concentration and increase their attention span.

By nature, play is *self-correcting learning* — every educator's dream. A child whose clay sculpture keeps falling over makes adjustments until he or she gets it right, thereby learning some basic principles of engineering while gaining some practice in problem-solving strategies.

Children thrive on play that requires them to *think*. That's why it's important to avoid overstructuring playtime. Parents should also avoid the all-too-common impulses to direct dramatic play, suggest adjustments in the construction of buildings, and recommend embellishments to art projects.

You can, however, help your child derive the maximum benefit from play activities by providing suitable toys, giving instruction in safety and care, and joining in when invited to do so.

Are there "right" and "wrong" toys? Child development specialists say no; children have differing tastes in toys, just as they do in everything else. But there are accepted guidelines you can use to choose toys that are most likely to provide your child with long-term amusement and opportunities for development.

• **A good toy is consistent with the values you wish to promote within your family.** If you're concerned about the level of violence in modern society, then you won't be comfortable with the kinds of play inspired by robots that shoot laser beams, tanks that demolish everything in their paths, and army figures (present or futuristic) equipped with arsenals of weaponry. Similarly, if the early sophistication of today's youth is a concern, Barbie and Ken and their jet-set accoutrements are probably not for your family.

It may be difficult to stand firm against Madison Avenue, but when a family comes to terms with what will and will not be accepted, everyone is more comfortable. Each family must arrive at its own compromises. As one four-year-old explained to his grandmother, "Michael can have G.I. Joe because he's fighting for his country, but he can't have He-Man 'cause he fights anybody. Angie can have everything, G.I. Joe and He-Man and Voltron. Christopher can't have any of those guys because his family *never* likes shooting or bombing or bashing. Sometimes Christopher shoots with his finger, though. I can have swords but not guns. Guns are for shooting people but swords are just used in contests, so nobody gets dead."

- **A good toy is safely and sturdily constructed.** Not only is it harmless when used as intended, but the manufacturer has also considered the alternatives. In other words, it is also harmless when it is abused.

This is an especially important consideration for parents of very bright children, whose drive to know the whys and wherefores of everything may cause them to examine their playthings rather creatively. One two-year-old nearly destroyed her digestive system with an inflated "baby bopper" designed to pop up when bashed down. Little windows in the plastic sides gave a clear view of several BB-sized red balls. Early one Saturday morning the child found a screwdriver, performed surgery on the "kid-proof" vinyl, and was on the verge of swallowing a handful of the balls when her parents discovered her.

- **A good toy is interactive.** It lets your child become involved with it in some significant way. Mechanized critters and cars may be appealing in the store, but they don't do much to sustain interest. The toys you choose should be designed so that the *child* does the moving and decision-making, not the toy.

- **A good toy is versatile.** Actually, any toy is versatile in that a child will probably come up with many more uses for it than the manufacturer originally intended. Looking for a toy that is *naturally* versatile is still important, however, in that it is often the best buy for the money.

A battery-powered dog that blinks, sits up, and begs is probably an expensive item. And what's the point if after a couple of weeks of being packed in toy airplanes, used as a bloodhound in police chases, and stashed behind the toilet for hide-and-seek, its eyes are dull and lifeless and its fur is worn off? Better to start with a less flashy but more durable animal.

- **A good toy is matched to the abilities and interests of the child.** Remember that the abilities of high-potential children may not develop according to the typical timeline. Toys chosen according to the age levels printed on the boxes may prove uninteresting after the first ten minutes.

On the other hand, it's not practical to routinely purchase toys intended for older children. These may require small muscle coordination a younger child doesn't have, or lack the safety features appropriate for him or her. Just because children have the intellect to understand a game involving many small pieces doesn't mean they will have the maturity to keep track of them or the sense to keep them out of their various orifices.

☐ ■ ☐

Early childhood educators who make home visits comment on how much they can tell about an environment by the kinds of toys they find there. Often parents don't even realize that they are promoting one-sided behavior in their children by their choice of toys.

One home we visited had only "educational" toys in the playroom — games to teach adding and subtracting, science lab kits, authentic dinosaur models, and how-to books. There were no stuffed animals, art materials, trucks, or works of fiction. The parents were vocal about the fact that their children had only the "best" toys, yet they had requested the visit because neither of their children seemed to fit in around the neighborhood. Their son was known to the other first-graders as the "little professor," and the parents had completely missed seeing the connection between his play environment and his unusual social behaviors.

This is not to say that an environment featuring a variety of toys will automatically produce a well-rounded child. For gifted children, this issue is more complex. Some prefer to focus on one type of toy to the exclusion of all others, and it's a battle to divert them long enough to try anything else. Nevertheless, it will pay off in the long run to encourage (not force) a variety of play activities. Even if your mad scientist doesn't choose to draw when left to her own devices, she may consider joining in if you start using crayons, cloth swatches, glue, and glitter to depict a laboratory experiment. Remember that your child loves you and wants to be with you; if you make it clear that you're available for play, you'll probably have a playmate.

☐ ■ ☐

Your child's toybox should contain both active and quiet-time toys. There should be items that stimulate symbolic play, intellectual development, risk-taking, social interaction, physical development, language proficiency, and spatial perspective.

Symbolic play occurs when something — an object, a sound, a mental image — is used to represent something else and comes to symbolize it. Symbolic play is crucial to overall development for a number of reasons. To participate, a child must make certain intellectual connections — good exercise for an integrated brain. Pretending to become an animal or drive a car requires the child to pull together everything he or she knows about that creature or thing. The child must analyze its purpose, the way it moves, its environment, and the noises it makes. Developmentally delayed children have been known to raise their I.Q. scores when they are systematically encouraged to play "let's pretend."

Symbolic play is also a necessary prelude to reading, as it helps a child to realize that one thing can stand for another. That concept must be grasped before the child can go on to understand that a group of letters is a symbol for a sound, and that sound is a symbol for an object or an idea. Math, too, is dependent on an understanding of numbers as symbols for groups of things.

"I don't know if I like playing Mr. Mom."

Many aspects of symbolic play also encourage both language and social development. Playing house, for example, allows children to take on the roles of other family members and experience empathy for their needs and concerns. Any play in which a child pretends to be someone else also encourages vocabulary development and practice in communication.

Finally, symbolic play is good for a child's emotional health. In certain play situations, children use objects or situations as symbols for things that frighten or disturb them, thereby working through their anxieties. A child facing a hospital visit can fantasize about the experience with a toy medical kit and some willing friends or stuffed animals to play "doctors" and "nurses."

Toys that stimulate symbolic and fantasy play include:
- Dolls and all their props (blankets, carriages, bottles, etc.)
- Movable action figures
- Little plastic people
- Stuffed or plastic animals
- Dress-up clothes
- Medical kits, tool kits, tools of any trade
- Telephones, play intercoms, paper-cup-and-string walkie-talkies
- Hats of all shapes and sizes
- Face paints
- Toy vehicles
- A wide and varied set of art supplies
- Blocks and building sets (Tinker Toys, DUPLOs, LEGOs)
- Puppets

Toys that purport to stimulate *intellectual development* might be more accurately described as promoting academic development. Fantasy, creativity, spatial development, and social growth are all aspects of the intellect, so virtually any toy which addresses these areas may be said to engage a child in intellectual development.

There are many toys that have been designed specifically to promote the kinds of behaviors in children that will later help them in school. They include:
- Lotto games
- Games that require the child to sequence items or ideas
- Shape-sorting toys
- Cuisenaire rods (the commercial equivalent of the colored straws described on page 100 of the Math Activities section)
- Automated quiz games (See and Spell; the Sesame Street Cookie Counter)

- Knowledge testers, like Go to the Head of the Class or Tot Trivia
- Clocks
- Globes
- Aquariums
- Terrariums
- Scales
- Microscopes
- Telescopes
- Binoculars

Certain toys help to encourage appropriate *risk-taking behavior* in young children. As avoidance of risk-taking is sometimes a problem for older gifted children, parents might consider making a special effort to provide items from this category.

A toy which promotes risk-taking is one which allows more than one way to accomplish a task and offers satisfaction for successful completion without exacting consequences for mistakes. This sounds complicated, but the most simple playthings fall into this category.

For example, modeling clay is ideal. The child has the opportunity to try out a number of ideas, and failure is just one more step on the road to success. If a mistake is made when modeling a figure, the offending portion may be nipped off and alterations made. If the whole piece doesn't make it, no harm done — simply squash it down and start on something else.

Other toys of this type include:

- Games of chance
- Building materials
- Puzzles
- Basic chemistry sets
- Art materials

Certain toys encourage both *physical development* and development of *spatial perspective*. Young children need ample opportunities for both small- and large-muscle exercise. They need to experiment with their bodies in time and space, as well as to manipulate objects within these same parameters. Especially for children who don't excel in physical activity, the best toys and games are those which are noncompetitive.

Bright children are accustomed to doing things well and may avoid situations in which they cannot excel. Then they become even less proficient at such activities, and they're suddenly caught in a vicious circle. Although many older gifted kids claim to disdain "jock stuff," a healthier attitude is to find appropriate methods of exercise that are nonthreatening and even fun.

It's never too early to promote a sense of enjoyment in one's physical development. Three- to five-year-olds should have access to the following large-muscle exercisers:

- Creative playground equipment suitable for climbing, jumping, and riding (it's not necessary to buy it; instead, walk, ride a bike, or even drive to good playgrounds)
- Large, hollow cardboard blocks for building, pushing, carrying, and shoving
- Pounding toys
- Toss games such as horseshoes (plastic or rubber), ringtoss, or beanbag toss
- A balance beam, low to the ground at first (two cement blocks and a sturdy, smooth board will do)
- Riding toys, both those that use feet and those that use pedals for locomotion
- A wagon
- Balls of all sizes

Small-muscle exercisers include:

- Puzzles
- Shape sorters
- DUPLOs or LEGOs
- Model kits (with fairly large parts)
- Art supplies
- Games that require balancing items on top of one another.

Sources for Hard-to-Find Toys, Games, and Equipment

The following catalogs offer an alternative to shopping malls and discount stores, which often contain little more than the toys currently starring in Saturday-morning cartoons. Some represent companies with lines of toys designed for home use; others are from companies that sell primarily to schools and other institutions. We include the latter because they also have significant sections of materials that you could use in your home, and the companies are willing to fill small orders to individual parties.

Before sending or telephoning for any of these, consider these two caveats: First, you may feel an overwhelming temptation to start buying all kinds of fancy workbooks and "official learning tools" that really are more appropriate for large-group use. Take a moment to remind yourself about the dangers of subjecting young children to formal instruction in lieu of quality free play. Second, once you have ordered from a catalog, prepare for a deluge of unsolicited ones. Companies sell their mailing lists, and your name may end up on several.

Kaplan School Supply Corporation
600 Jonestown Road
PO Box 15027
Winston-Salem, NC 27103
1-800-334-2014 (in North Carolina, 1-800-642-0610; main office, 919/768-4450)
Primarily school supplies, but also includes many medium-priced quality toys. Also has a few toy storage systems in the affordable range for home use.

Constructive Playthings (Home Edition)
1227 East 199th Street
Grandview, MO 64030
1-800-255-6124
(In Missouri, 816/761-5900)
Colorful and appealing medium-priced toys, many standard, some unusual. If you live in Kansas, California, Texas, or Illinois, you may want to shop one of their stores.

Toys To Grow On
2695 E. Dominguez St.
PO Box 17
Long Beach, CA 90801-0017
213/603-8890
The best of the bunch for a
child's wish list. It has some
unusual offerings, some old
standbys, and some fancy filler
as well. Once you're on the
mailing list, you receive seasonal
updates. If you've got a poor
memory and many children's
birthdays to buy for, you can
even join their birthday club.
They'll send you a reminder in
advance of each birthday, along
with a list of suggestions.

**Playtime Equipment and School
Supply, Inc.**
808 Howard St.
Omaha, NE 68102
402/345-1546
An exceptionally thick catalog of
educational materials, many but
not all suitable for home use. The
largest choice of puzzles you are
likely to find anywhere.

**The Growing Years: Childcraft
Early Childhood and School
Catalog**
20 Kilmer Road
CN 066
Edison, NJ 08818
1-800-631-5652
(In New Jersey, 201/572-6100)
A staple for schools and daycare
centers, this also offers toys,
books, and a few other assorted
items for homes.
(Minimum order: $20.00.)

Presents for the Promising
Box 134
Sewell, NJ 08080
An offshoot of the *Gifted Children
Newsletter,* this small catalog
features items preselected to
appeal to promising children of
all ages.

Educational Teaching Aids
159 West Kinzie St.
Chicago, IL 60610
312/559-1400
Primarily institutional, but does
have some interesting puzzles,
construction sets, and art
materials.

CHAPTER 7

Making the Most of Your Home Computer

During the last few years, microcomputers have become the third largest selling home commodity — after houses themselves and cars. One way advertisers have helped this to happen is by filling parents with anxiety and guilt. You know the ads: A toddler sits at a computer, happily keystroking away, while the announcer strongly hints that if *you* want to ensure *your* child's future success in school, you had better buy a computer. Or a young, overweight, unattractive boy sadly steps off the bus into his parents' arms, having just been kicked out of prep school because he *didn't* have a computer.

How much truth is there to all of this hype? The answer is...some. Computer use with young children can certainly be one factor in an appropriately enriched environment, but it's not going to ensure early entrance into the Harvard Business School. While computers can aid in teaching thinking and learning skills, they offer virtually nothing that can't be accomplished by an even marginally creative parent, *sans* software. In other words, they're nice but not necessary to have.

It would be silly to invest in a home computer specifically for use by young children. But for those of us who already have them or plan to purchase them for other reasons, there's no reason why we can't also share them with our preschoolers.

Each day, new educational software hits the market, so how can you choose those packages that are best for your child? Some of what's out there is good, but a fair proportion is junk. By its very nature, the computer is a vehicle for electronic wizardry. While this can enhance many kinds of learning, it can also effectively mask the fact that a program billed as "educational" may actually be a lot of show and very little substance. And given that you often have to buy before you try, mistakes can get expensive.

There are two major categories in educational software. A program may provide *drill-and-practice,* or it may provide *problem-solving opportunities.*

Drill-and-practice programs contain repetitive activities which emphasize letter recognition, matching, counting, ordering of letters and numbers, and the like. Because these type of programs are easiest to write, there are many such packages available. Their chief value is that they provide immediate and appealing feedback to the user. The chief drawback is that too much drill-and-practice is inappropriate for young children.

Problem-solving programs ask the child to use logic to reach a certain end. Good ones will introduce a concept to the child and then provide a variety of applications in which the concept must be used to solve a problem. These, too, are capable of providing immediate feedback. But because they are harder to write, they are also harder to find.

A 1985 study done by Sherman, Divine, and Johnson of Eastern New Mexico University found that when preschool children were given a choice between drill-and-practice and problem-solving programs, they overwhelmingly preferred the latter.* Let this be your guide when choosing software for your child.

Before purchasing any package, ask to try it out in the store. (Depending on where you buy it, this may be possible. Computer stores are a better bet than discount stores, although the discounters' return policies may be more generous.) Evaluate its ease of use and look to see if the accompanying manual provides strategies for teaching the program to your child.

An adaptation of the characteristics Sherman, Divine, and Johnson used when comparing the two kinds of software can also prove helpful to you when shopping. Whether you're considering a drill-and-practice or a problem-solving package, try rating each of these characteristics (when applicable) on a continuum from awful to excellent:

— **Animation.** In an animated program, the figures and objects on the display terminal move, either on their own or when prompted by the child. Is the animation interesting, novel, meaningful or just showy?

— **Color.** Some programs require a color monitor, and children tend to prefer programs with color in them. Again, how is it used?

— **Closure.** Is an ending provided for the program, or does it keep running until the child chooses to stop? Opinion is divided on which is best, but we lean toward the former.

— **Reinforcement.** How is the child "rewarded" for correct responses? Some programs include sound, music, building a picture, animation, letting the child play a game, etc.

— **Teaching/prompting.** How does the program react to an incorrect response? Does it immediately provide the answer, or give clues to help the child reach it on his or her own?

— **Levels of difficulty and complexity.** Will the program grow with your child?

Following are some programs other parents have recommended. The grade levels listed are suggested by the manufacturers and may or may not apply to your child.

---

* Janice Sherman, Katherine Divine, and Betty Johnson, "An Analysis of Computer Software Preferences of Preschool Children," *Educational Technology* (May 1985), pages 39-41.

Recommended Hardware and Software

Muppet Learning Keys Keyboard. Grades preschool-1. (64K Apple IIe, IIc; Commodore 64; 128K IBM PCjr.) A keyboard specially designed for young children, with numbers and letters in sequential (rather than QWERTY) order. Comes with three software programs to teach letter, number, and picture recognition.

Muppetville. Grades preschool-1. (64K Apple IIe, IIc. Works with Apple Mouse, Touch Window, or Muppet Learning Keys.) Muppet characters offer activities in identifying and classifying shapes, colors, and numbers.

Odd One Out. Grades K-6. (48K Apple II⁺, IIe, IIc; Commodore 64. Color monitor required. Works with Touch Window.) Develops classification skills. The child is shown four items and asked to identify the "odd one out." Increasing levels of difficulty.

Iggy's Gnees. Grades 1-4. (48K Apple II⁺, IIe, IIc. Color monitor required. Works with Muppet Learning Keys.) Builds visual discrimination skills. The child examines groups of shapes, one containing examples of "gnees," the other examples of "not gnees," and tries to determine what the rule is that defines gnees. Increasing levels of complexity.

Mr. Pixel's Cartoon Kit. (Commodore 64.) Children design and assemble their own cartoons. A visual menu is always available at the bottom of the screen, so with training even young children can create basic cartoons. Increasing levels of complexity.

Getting Ready to Read and Add. Grades preschool-1. (48K Apple II⁺, IIe, IIc; 16K Atari 400, 800XL series joystick or paddle optional; Commodore 64; 64K IBM PC or 128K IBM PCjr.)

Learning with Leeper. Preschool and up. (Apple II, II⁺, IIe. Color monitor required.) Leeper is a critter who offers games in counting, letter and shape recognition, maze solving, and screen painting.

Teddy's Playground. Grades K-4. (48K Apple II⁺, IIe, IIc. Color monitor required. Works with Apple Mouse and Muppet Learning Keys.) Develops critical thinking skills by allowing children to manipulate attributes in games with Teddy at his playground.

Dinosaur Dig. (Apple II, Commodore 64, IBM PC.) This package capitalizes on young children's fascination with dinosaurs. It illustrates and discusses two dozen dinosaurs and offers games to check mastery of material. A bit sophisticated, but fine for the true young enthusiast.

Magic Slate. Grades 2-adult. (48K Apple II⁺, IIe, IIc. Graphics printer desirable.) A word processing program suitable for use by young writers.

Stickybear ABC. Grades K-2. (Apple 48K, Commodore 64, Atari 48K.) Uses animated graphics to introduce letters and sounds. The graphics are exceptionally appealing, but the program is introductory only as it requires no response from the child.

Mask Parade. Grades K-6. (Apple 64K, IBM PC/PCjr. Printer required.) Children use elements of design to create paper masks, hats, badges, glasses, and jewelry.

Gertrude's Secrets. Grades K-4. (Apple II⁺ 48K. Color monitor required.) Gertrude the Goose shares her secrets regarding shapes and puzzles. Promotes spatial awareness.

Turtle Toyland Junior. (Coleco Adam, Commodore 64, IBM PC. Joystick required.) Introduces computer programming through the use of a joystick. Children can draw shapes, compose music, and combine various elements in "filmstrips."

Bumble Games. Grades K-4. (Apple II⁺ 48K. Color monitor required.) Teaches color and space relations to nonreaders. Also offers games to teach number lines, pairs, and graph plotting.

Story Tree. (Apple II.) Young children will probably need their parents' help with this one. The object is to create stories with many possible plot twists and conclusions.

Recommended Reading

Mindstorms: Children, Computers and Powerful Ideas by Seymour Papert (New York: Basic Books, Inc., 1982).

Computer books come and go with the speed of light, so check with your librarian or bookstore for the newest and latest offerings.

PART III

COPING
WITH THE SCHOOLS

CHAPTER 8

Choosing a Preschool

Some sort of early schooling is becoming the accepted pattern for increasing numbers of American families. Many children enter kindergarten as graduates of preschools, daycare, or organized play groups. Even those who have never regularly attended sessions without their parents have likely participated in parent-child classes. For some parents, registering for a special class — music, crafts, swimming, dance, whatever — represents one in a series of enriched opportunities they provide for their child. For others, full- or part-time child care is a necessity. Whichever applies to you, it's important to get the best possible care for your young son or daughter.

An alternative that works for one child may not be acceptable for another. What matters is whether your child and the program you choose make a good match. A proper fit between a child and early education experiences can help him or her to retain and enhance the love of learning all children are born with, while a poor fit can make a child miserable and a parent guilt-ridden.

Consider Timothy. As a three-year-old, he spent the school year in a supportive and enriched family daycare environment. Because the provider took the summers off, his working parents put Timothy into a highly recommended preschool for that three-month period.

The first days of excited anticipation about "real school" soon gave way to tearful mornings and evenings of acting up. Although the environment at the preschool was more structured and academic than his parents would have liked, it was obvious that the staff was dedicated to children and that other children were flourishing under their care. His parents decided that under the circumstances it was best to give everyone a chance to adjust; perhaps Timothy would learn some coping skills along the way. As the summer wore on, things did seem to improve, and although Timothy was never carefree in his attitude toward the school his negative behaviors disappeared and he even spoke enthusiastically of certain activities.

At the end of the three months it came time to assess the program and to decide whether to stay on or move to another setting. Timothy's mother sat him down and, as an introduction to the topic of his future, told him how proud she and Daddy were of his adjustment to the "big school." Timothy's answer was totally unexpected. "I don't let my face cry anymore," he said, "but my insides still cry every day."

This story has an almost happy ending. The discussion went no further, Timothy was returned to a family daycare setting, and within a couple of months he was back to his old sunny self. A full year later, though, he is still insisting that he will never go to school again but will stay in daycare until he grows up to be a dad. While his parents hesitate to overemphasize the significance of a short-lived and adequately handled incident, they would rather have skipped this mess altogether. Childhood has enough built-in stress, and parenting enough built-in guilt.

It is important to note that the problems Timothy experienced were not a result of early education *per se* (as evidenced by his thriving in another environment), but of a poor match between his need for personal attention and flexibility and the center's need for formal instruction and structure. Under the right circumstances there is no question but that early education can offer a child many rewards.

For the purposes of this discussion, let's stop drawing distinctions between daycare and preschool. Because young children are so new at life, *all* that they do can be considered "early learning." While one environment may call itself one thing and another something else, the labels are less significant than what actually goes on during the time the child attends. We have observed family "daycare" settings where the provider was a born teacher and her charges were benefiting from the best and most current early education strategies, and we have seen "nursery schools" that were nothing more than group babysitting arrangements. It is not a question of whether early education occurs under one structure or another, but of what kind of education takes place.

The education your child receives outside your home can be grouped into the same developmental categories as the education you as a parent provide.

Emotional and Social Skills Development

The evidence is clear that a child's awareness of social conventions, sociability, and ability to cooperate with parents, other adults, and other children are all affected by daycare and preschool experiences.

This is especially true for young gifted children. Most of their feelings about their abilities will come from their parents and the group experiences they have. If the environment does not value what they can do but instead works to make them behave more "typically," they will likely develop self-esteem problems fairly early in the game. On the other hand, if they are in a setting in which they are head and shoulders above their agemates in many areas of development, they are at risk for *over*estimating their abilities. Many gifted children have trouble handling competition, and this may stem in part from the fact that they had none during preschool and primary school. They may grow to confuse "good work" with "being the best" and continue to operate from this erroneous standard for years.

We have seen first-graders come unglued when classmates completed more items on a timed math test than they did. It didn't matter that both scores were excellent; what mattered was that they had been "beaten." An appropriately structured early school environment can help to obviate some of these potential problems.

Cognitive Skills Development

While the jury is still out regarding the question of which makes for smarter (or less smart) children, home care or daycare, there is clearcut evidence that the *quality* of the outside care affects the overall ability of children to think and reason. This, too, has special significance for children of special ability. As noted in Chapter 4, young minds are very plastic and are profoundly influenced by their environment. Therefore, it is logical to assume that if a bright child is in a setting that stimulates most other children but leaves him or her cold, that child's brain will not develop as it otherwise might.

Specialists in early childhood development maintain that the ages of ten months to two years are critical to intellectual growth. During this period, children need lots of stimulation, both sensory and intellectual. In her book, *Growing Up Gifted: Developing the Potential of Children at Home and at School,* Dr. Barbara Clark recommends the following caregiver activities and gives a rationale for each type.

If you are at home a great deal with your child, you can provide these kinds of stimulation yourself. But if your child is away from you for a large part of each workday, you should make sure that your daycare provider does as many of the following as possible.

Caregiver Activities:	Because:
Organize and design a safe physical environment that allows for a variety of sensory experiences; family living areas and outdoor areas should be available for exploration of the senses:	Toddlers spend most of their time gaining information, building concepts, and observing.

Visual: plants, fish in bowls, pictures, patterned objects, mirrors

Auditory: exposure to many types of music, voices, rhythms, singing, bells, drums, shakers, music boxes, animal sounds

Tactile: a variety of textures to feel (soft, hard, rough, smooth), sculpture, finger food, mud play, finger paints, painting with jello

Olfactory: baking smells, flower smells, farm and field smells

Gustatory: snacks of differing tastes and textures

Caregiver Activities:	Because:
Provide a variety of toys and household objects to play with: for stringing, nesting, digging, pounding, screwing; construction toys (pieces not too small), peg boards, record players, magnets, magnetic letters, alphabet blocks, prisms, water toys, flashlights, spin tops, jigsaw puzzles, magnifying glasses, dolls, collections of small objects, toy animals, various household tools, books, and art materials.	This gives intellectual stimulation, support for later learning, strengthens perception and problem-solving abilities.
Play games like hide-n-seek, treasure hunts, guessing games, matching and sorting, finger games, circle games; encourage and provide materials for imitative play, such as "I do what you do."	This facilitates concept development, practice in planning and carrying out complicated projects, anticipating consequences, developing skills of problem solving.
Teach child to be aware of and name objects in the environment (including baby's own body parts). This can be done by playing games with the caregiver, giving names to objects as they are used.	This provides language experience.
Look at scrapbooks with child, read books to child, make books familiar.	This provides symbolic language experiences.
Make scrapbooks with the child of pictures of animals, cars, trips. These can become the child's own books.	This gives language experience.

Caregiver Activities:	Because:
Talk to baby during all caregiving activities: bathing, dressing, eating; use patterns of speech with baby that you use with other members of the family; short twenty to thirty second "conversations" are important.[1]	This helps baby to understand more complicated sentences, increases language background and experience.
Take neighborhood walks to library, stores, playgrounds, on collection excursions, out to feed birds; always discuss what is seen and experienced.	This provides a background of experiences for future concept building.

Dr. Clark's admonition against too much babytalk is well taken. In our experience, intelligent children neither appreciate it nor respond to it.

Consider Jonah. When he was around two years old, his mother trotted him off for an official "portrait" at a local photographer's studio. The photographer immediately started using babytalk on him. She sat him down, waggled a stuffed animal in front of his face, and went behind the camera, all the while speaking a stream of nonsense.

---

[1]Note. When engaging children in "conversation" try to talk about what they are doing from their perspective. Try to understand their meaning for the activity and what they may be learning from it. Then try to give them something new and interesting to think about along the same lines. Allow children to initiate the activity and then respond enthusiastically, but be careful not to insist on doing it only your way.

Also use language to heighten curiosity and develop interest. Teach children vocabulary words to express their interests by engaging them at the point of interest. This will further help children see adults as valuable resources. Talk to your child even before you are sure the child understands what you are saying. It is important to use a variety of speech patterns and normal conversational intonations. Remember, you are the model. While the act of repeating sounds the baby makes is fun and can be enjoyed by both adult and baby, the child needs good speech models and language patterns. Babytalk does not provide a useful model for children to emulate. Children do create unusual patterns for their own use. However, repetition of these patterns by the adult limits children to these unique patterns.

Jonah got up and walked toward his mother. The photographer came out from behind the camera, sat him back down, repeated the stuffed animal routine, and moved toward the camera, still talking babytalk. Jonah got up again.

"Coo chi coo... how about a BIG Smiley poo..."

This sequence occurred once more before the photographer, exasperated, turned to Jonah's mother and asked, "Why won't he sit there? I keep asking him to sit there." Jonah's mother replied, "I honestly don't think he understands you. We don't talk babytalk to him."

"Jonah," said the photographer, looking at the boy, "will you please sit on the chair? Just for a minute?"

"Okay," Jonah replied, and sat. And stayed relatively still for the five minutes the photographer needed.

Moral Development

Dr. Clark quotes research indicating that children begin to show differences in altruistic behavior between the ages of 18 and 24 months. Dr. Paul MacLean, who developed the triune brain model, goes so far as to suggest that early exercise in altruism and empathy is necessary for the development of the neural pathways that allow for this behavior. Children who are taught respect for others, and are themselves respected, will develop the faculties needed for moral behavior more readily than those who are harshly punished or permitted to be completely self-involved in the preschool years.

There is ample anecdotal evidence that gifted children develop this sense of empathy early, so this should be an important consideration in choosing early school experiences for such children. Nursery school staff who deal with very sensitive youngsters need to be aware that while some three-year-olds must be encouraged to take another person's point of view, others have to be helped to put their already highly-developed sensitivity into perspective.

Four-year-old Tammy spent an entire Christmas season worrying during every rendition of "Rudolph, the Red-Nosed Reindeer" that Rudolph was lonely and unloved. Whether she heard it on the elevator, the car radio, or in a school concert, when it came to the lines about Rudolph being called names and left out of games, Tammy anxiously asked, "But not anymore, right?" Four-and-a-half-year-old Sean burst into tears the first time he heard "Away in a Manger." He wanted to know why baby Jesus had to sleep on hay, and why the stars were staring at him.

The point is that such children need an especially responsive environment if they are to come to terms with the realities of life in a way that is neither unrealistically protective nor damagingly harsh. Caregivers should be willing to deal gently with a child's fears and patiently model sharing and caring behaviors.

Finding The Preschool That Fits Your Child

So how do you go about finding the best setting for your child? TV and radio announcers and magazine writers tell us weekly about the terrible shortage of good child care, yet there seem to be almost too many choices available. Do you want half-day, full-day, or every-other-day care? Is it better to choose a franchise, a university lab school, a church center, or a family setting? Or should you go ahead and start your own co-op?

And what about philosophy? Which is preferable — a Piagetian base, the Montessori method, or the Sullivan approach?

It's enough to make you stay home and watch "Sesame Street" together. As one mother put it after interviewing 15 prospective daycare providers, "Well, my daughter can either be safe all day and bored out of her mind, or be stimulated and in danger of her life every minute."

Your first step should be to determine your purpose for sending your child to preschool. The most obvious may be the need to have your child cared for while you and your spouse are away at work, but there should be more to it than that. Specifically: Do you want the setting to extend the kinds of activities and experiences you provide at home, or would you rather it complement what you already provide?

Some parents of bright and talented children want the preschool to take up where the home leaves off in terms of instruction. For them, a setting which offers a great deal of free play and only the most basic instruction is a poor choice. They will not be comfortable unless the child shows some intellectual progress, so they should find a program that focuses on academic skills development.

Other parents with equally bright and talented children may welcome the free play environment because it stimulates social development. They view it as their responsibility to provide the intellectual stimulation and consider the tuition money well spent if their kids spend their mornings in the sandbox.

Obviously no child will benefit from a setting where the values are radically different from those found in his or her home. Many Christian parents have put Christian values at the top of their list of requirements when looking for daycare; many daycare providers are making their church affiliations known. Ethnic background may also be influential.

Once you have decided what you want your child's preschool to be — an extension of what you're doing at home, or something complementary — you can get down to shopping and selecting. There are five basic steps involved in this process:

1. Talking to other parents about what they've found, liked, and disliked,

2. Checking with local referral services and county licensing bureaus,

3. Interviewing directors and/or staff members,

4. Observing the program in operation, and

5. Making up your mind.

During your interviews, be careful to ask questions that are neutral and open-ended rather than leading. For example, a question like, "You don't sacrifice individuality for structure, do you?" can only have one possible answer, and of course it will be the one you're hoping to hear. But it won't teach you anything. Instead, try, "Tell me some specific ways you provide for the needs of individual children," followed by, "Now please share some ways in which you meet the needs of the children as a group." This approach is more likely to yield a true picture of the program's philosophy.

There are many technical terms for varying philosophies, but when the jargon is pushed aside most programs can be evaluated according to where they fall on the following continua.

Child centered ←——————→ Teacher centered

Activities and resources are provided; children choose from among them

Instructors guide groups of children through prescribed units and activities

Spontaneous activity ←——————→ Structured activity

Free play is encouraged; teachers take their cues from children in planning instruction

Teachers carefully plan activities to produce desired learning outcomes

Enrichment ←——————→ Acceleration

Bright children are encouraged to expand their learning through exploration of new topics or of familiar topics in new ways

Bright children are encouraged to advance briskly through skills areas, like math and reading

Life skills ←——————→ Academic skills

Emphasis is on social and emotional growth

Emphasis is on expanding the child's knowledge base and intellectual skills development

Because there is so much to be said for a well-balanced program, most espouse philosophies somewhere in the middle of each continuum. In practice, however, many land far to the left or the right in most categories. For example, one nursery school claimed to offer training for life skills and academic skills in equal measure. The life skills activities, however, consisted of learning how to shake hands and perform formal introductions — behaviors few four-year-olds need or care about. For the rest of the day, the children practiced writing and similar pursuits. The program sounded appropriate for very bright children, but in reality it was better suited for socially inept adults.

When observing a program, what should you watch for? Dr. Bryna Siegel-Gorelick suggests two ways to structure your observation so as to pick up on any discrepancies between theory and practice: *person-focused observation* and *event sampling.**

---

* Bryna Siegel-Gorelick, *The Working Parents' Guide to Child Care* (Boston: Little, Brown & Co., 1983), page 132.

Person-focused observation involves choosing one child or one teacher (better yet, one of each) and watching that individual closely over a period of time.

If your own child is of exceptional ability, spend a few moments discreetly searching the room for a child who seems to be ahead of the norm in some area. (He or she need not have the same kinds of ability as your child.) Then concentrate your attention on that individual, keeping these questions in mind:

- How does he spend his time?
- Is she self-directed, or does she constantly look to the teacher for guidance?
- Is he able to reach materials and supplies for himself, or is it necessary to ask the teacher for assistance?
- If a conflict occurs, to whom does she turn to for help in resolution — herself, another child, or the teacher?
- Are his activities primarily social or academic in nature?
- Over the course of a half-hour, how many activities is she involved in?
- Does he work alone or in a group?
- To what degree does her conversation with other children involve comments on ability? Are the comments positive ("I like your picture") or negative ("That's dumb. Cats only have one tail")?

After you have finished observing this one child, go back to the continua and quickly make "x's" at the points on each that you feel were reflected in the child's behavior. Don't spend a lot of time on this; just follow your gut feelings.

Next, turn your attention to a staff member. Try to discover answers to these questions:

- Does the teacher build on children's stories and pictures?
- Does he ask provocative questions or suggest his own embellishments?
- Does she frequently call groups of children to her for instruction?
- Is the entire class focused on him, or does he circle the room, watching the various activities and intervening only when necessary? Does he ever intervene before you think it's necessary?

- Who initiates most student-teacher interactions — the children, or the teacher?
- Which gets the larger share of his time — problem behaviors, or acceptable behaviors?
- Does she "catch" students doing something right and praise them as often as she "catches" them doing something wrong and offers correction?
- Does he spend more time with children who are working, or with children who are playing?

What you see will yield a second set of "x's" on the continua. Again, jot these down quickly; don't intellectualize or second-guess yourself. Your initial responses will be the most honest, and you will probably return to them again and again.

Since your chances of finding a program that lands smack in the middle of every continuum are fairly slim, in which direction should you lean, left or right? That's entirely up to you. In our experience, however, the preferred environment for gifted and talented children seems to be slightly to the left of center.

Dr. Siegel-Gorelick's second technique, event sampling, involves what it implies: watching how the children and the teacher behave during several "events," or unscheduled activities. Look for the kinds of events common to groups of young children (such as fighting over toys), but also be alert to those that parallel the concerns you have for your own child.

For example, if your bright youngster is troubled by social situations, watch for an incident in which one child is attempting to enter a play activity already in progress. How successful is the child in his or her attempts to be recognized and gain access? If the child is rejected, is the teacher aware of it? What strategies are offered by the teacher to help solve the problem? Does the teacher attempt to legislate a solution or coach the children to work one out for themselves?

You might also watch for a situation in which one child is attempting to organize a play activity that is too complicated for the others to handle. How does the child try to convince the others to participate? How does he or she communicate the "rules" of the activity? How does he or she respond when (or if) rejected by the others?

During all of your observations, remember that your purpose is to determine whether the setting will be a good fit for your child, not to judge the behavior of the teacher or the philosophy of the school. By keeping your eyes, ears, and mind open, you will glean much valuable information, but there is also much you will not pick up the first or even second time around.

For instance, let's say that the teacher did not seem aware when a child was rejected by a play group. Rather than judge her as inattentive, use what you saw as the basis for initiating a conversation (later, please, when she is not responsible for the children). Maintain a neutral demeanor and don't imply what you think she should have done. Simply describe the situation as you saw it, ask if she noticed, and then ask her to share her thoughts on similar situations. You may find that she has no strategies for this kind of thing — or that she provided the children with coaching in the past and was giving them the opportunity to act on her suggestions.

Remember, too, that no individual or program is perfect. Like parents, teachers have off days. You can assume that as paid professionals they will try to minimize the effect these will have on the children in their charge, but it's unreasonable to expect them all to be Mary Poppins.

How long the program has been in operation, and how long the children have been involved, can also make a difference. A new program, or an established program that has just accepted many new children, will run less smoothly than one where all hands are experienced. It may have the potential, however, to become precisely what you're looking for.

Should you bring your child to the observation sessions? If possible, yes. Just be aware that you can't necessarily count on him or her to provide you with valuable input. Some children can explain their feelings quite clearly, while others are somewhat cryptic.

Four-year-old Susan was adamant in her preference for one preschool over another. Her reason for disliking the first? "They make the kids write sevens all the time." Her reason for liking the second? "They hardly ever make anyone write sevens."

Finally: There has been so much in the news in recent years about daycare centers where horrible things happen that we feel compelled to say a few words about that. First, the vast majority of daycare providers are concerned and dedicated individuals. They put in long hours for distressingly low pay, and many stick with their profession for years. But none of this means that you shouldn't take every possible precaution to ensure that your child doesn't end up in danger.

There's one rule of thumb we live by: *If the school or center has certain hours during the day when parents are not allowed in their children's rooms, look elsewhere.* Not even naptimes or "quiet times" should be off limits. You as a parent have the right to drop in whenever you please, uninvited and unannounced.

After you've made your choice, exercise this right. Pay a few "surprise" visits at different times during different days spread out over several weeks. Don't deliberately disrupt the routine; it may be sufficient simply to poke your head in the door, nod hello to the teacher, see where your child is, and leave. If your child sees you, you may need to spend a few minutes with him or her, and he or she may scream when you get up to go. That's a small price to pay for knowing that your child is safe and protected.

Depending on your work schedule, you may want to get involved as a parent volunteer. Preschools often need extra bodies for trips to the zoo or the neighborhood park. Not only will this give you the opportunity to learn more about the teacher; you'll also be able to watch your child relate to his or her peers. Plus your child will be thrilled and pleased by your presence — and you may even have fun.

Choosing a Preschool: A Checklist

Once you have completed your focused observations, allow yourself time to view the Big Picture. The following questions have been adapted from a list compiled by the Gifted Center of the Educational Cooperative Services Unit/Twin Cities Metro Area in Minnesota. They are designed to reflect a concern for a good basic preschool environment, as well as one which is appropriate for high-potential children. (Few preschools are designed expressly for gifted children, although this appears to be changing in some major metropolitan areas.)

About the Staff

☐   Do teachers have degrees or training in early childhood education?

☐   What are the opportunities for staff in-service and training?

☐   How frequently are reports made to parents about children's progress?

☐   Are parents welcome to observe classes?

☐   Are children greeted individually as they arrive, and are they acknowledged as they leave?

☐   Is the language used by staff members appropriate and not patronizing?

☐   Do staff members walk around the room and speak to children directly instead of sitting at a desk and calling across the room?

☐   Are children addressed by their individual names instead of collectively?

☐   Do teachers ask questions which encourage creative thinking? (Not only "What happened?" but also "How and why did it happen?" and "What other ways might Mike have solved the problem?" or "How might the story have ended differently?")

☐   What is the attitude toward individual differences? Do teachers avoid comparing children and holding one or another up as role models? Or — even worse — as bad examples?

☐   How is discipline handled? Are encouragements offered for appropriate behavior? Do teachers try to redirect negative behavior more often than reprimand or punish?

☐   Is the staff membership consistent, or is the turnover rate high?

About the Students

☐   What is the range of abilities among students? Do children get equal amounts of attention regardless of ability?

☐   Are activities and groupings determined solely by age, or are children allowed to move from group to group as their abilities and comfort levels allow?

☐ Do the children refer to one another by name, rather than "Hey, Kid" or as "that girl"?

☐ Do the children seem exuberant and spontaneous yet under control?

About the Program

☐ Are there opportunities for both group and independent work?

☐ Are the children encouraged to make choices within an appropriately structured framework?

☐ Are there opportunities for artistic expression as well as academic work and play experience?

☐ Do the pieces of student work on display reflect individuality, or are they all the same?

☐ Are there opportunities for both large and small muscle coordination activities?

☐ Are there many books, and are they easily available to children?

☐ Are those children who can read encouraged to do so?

☐ Is everyone read to regularly, regardless of ability to read?

☐ Are math-related materials available? Are they manipulative in nature rather than paper-and-pencil tasks?

☐ If a computer is available, is it used in conjunction with, rather than as a substitute for, instruction?

☐ Does the program allow for flexibility in scheduling?

About the Environment

☐ Are there open spaces so the children can move about freely?

☐ Are there secluded areas for private work and play?

☐ Does each child have at least one spot to call his or her own in which to store ongoing work?

☐ Are bathrooms and eating areas easily and safely accessible?

☐   Are rooms colorful and attractive without being over-stimulating?

☐   Is equipment sturdy, safe, and in good repair?

☐   Are materials located within the reach of children?

A Special Aside to Parents of Gifted Girls

Recent studies present discouraging evidence that gifted women have fared no better in their careers than other female college graduates. And according to Joyce Juntune, executive director of the National Association for Gifted Children, today's school girls are still struggling over many of the same hurdles that stopped the generation ahead of them from going further. Many girls cannot accept how smart they are, and their parents send mixed messages: Do well in school, but be popular and "normal," too.

Psychologist Barbara A. Kerr has written a fascinating book that's worth reading: *Smart Girls/Gifted Women* (Columbus: Ohio Psychology Publishing Co., 1986). She offers several suggestions for helping young girls to be their best selves — and stresses that preschool isn't too soon to start:

• Dress your daughter for active play, not sitting on the sidelines. Have her wear bold, bright, washable clothes rather than pale pastels.

• Avoid daycare centers and preschools that segregate children by sex. Find out how the providers and teachers feel about sex roles. If possible, find a center or school that has men as well as women teachers.

• When considering a daycare center or preschool, check to see that it has plenty of books and allows time for reading them, as well as individual time with puzzles, musical instruments, and artwork.

• Take advantage of any preschool program that interests your daughter — music lessons, karate, dance, acrobatics.

• Take any opportunity to expand sex-role models. Point out and challenge the limiting stereotypes on TV. Plan special visits to your place of work (this is for both Mom and Dad) and explain what you do.

- Choose nonsexist toys for home play.
- Let your daughter know that you're delighted by her gifts and talents.

What the studies are telling us is that we can't sit back and complacently believe that things have changed since we were children. They have — and they haven't. Parents must still play an active role in ensuring that their gifted daughters have every chance to succeed.

Recommended Reading

The following books provide highly detailed information about specific types of preschools and the history and philosophy of various programs. Each also points out that the stated claims of any organization are not as important as what actually happens when the kids arrive, so be sure to back up anything you read with personal on-site observation.

A Parents' Guide to Nursery Schools by Jean Curtis (New York: Random House, 1971).

How To Choose a Nursery School by Ada Anbar (Palo Alto, California: Pacific Books, 1982).

The Working Parents' Guide to Child Care by Bryna Siegel-Gorelick (Boston: Little, Brown & Co., 1983). Also recommended:

The Early Education Connection: An Instructional Resource for Teachers and Parents of Preschool and Kindergarten Children by Maurice D. and Eugenia M. Fisher (Manassas, Virginia: The Reading Tutorium, 1981). Intended more for practitioners than for parents, this book contains solid suggestions along with summaries on Froebel, Montessori, and Piaget.

CHAPTER 9

A Preschool Screening Primer

Preschool screening is a service that many school districts offer to families with children who will be entering kindergarten in the coming year (or first grade, in states which don't require kindergarten attendance). It's designed primarily to aid the districts in assessing the children they will soon be serving, and it's almost always voluntary.

If you're like most parents of high-potential preschoolers, you'll probably want to go ahead with it. Just don't expect too much. Many parents hope that preschool screening will help them to determine whether their children really are advanced, and some plan to use the results (if obtained soon enough) to make decisions about possible early entrance. But screening wasn't designed for these purposes. Instead, it helps educators to discover children with developmental *problems* who may benefit from early intervention techniques.

Although several different screening instruments are used throughout the country, they usually share similar characteristics: They can be given efficiently to large numbers of children in relatively short periods of time, they don't require large investments in complex or costly equipment, and their format is simple enough to allow them to be administered by laypersons. By nature, then, they are relatively crude. While they are adequate to good when it comes to flagging children who may need a second look — in other words, more observation and testing — they generally will *not* indicate whether a child is significantly ahead of his or her peers or possessed of any special ability. The ceiling is simply too low; some 90 percent of incoming school-age children are able to achieve satisfactorily most items on the tests.

What can you expect to happen at a preschool screening? That depends on your school district and the screening procedures and instruments it has chosen. You and your child may be met by one person who will handle the entire screening, or you may be guided to a number of different stations for the assessment of different skills. You will probably be asked to complete a form or two asking for basic biographical and/or health information, and you may also be asked to report on whether your child can or cannot perform certain tasks.

What will screening personnel be looking for? They will likely observe your child for signs of speech or language difficulty, hearing problems, motor skill deficits, and delayed social skills. Four-year-olds will be asked to demonstrate that they know their name and address, can recognize colors and shapes, and understand such concepts as under and over, first and last, and so on.

Most screening personnel have both training and experience. They are aware that the situation is contrived and that a child's performance does not necessarily reflect how he or she will do in school. They also recognize that this assessment, like any other, is useful only as far as it goes: it is one in a series of indicators, not the final word.

Where such personnel tend to fall short is in the area of gifted young children. A very few school districts are beginning to realize that preschool screening provides an opportunity to look for children on *both* ends of the spectrum, but most still do not acknowledge the need to watch for special abilities or talents. What this means is that it's up to you to be alert to what goes on and any possible implications.

The following tips can help you to make the most of the screening process:

1. DON'T use it as a forum for explaining your child's giftedness. Certainly the school district needs to be aware of your concerns and the knowledge you have about your child, but the screening is not the best place to start imparting this information — unless the examiner is a practicing psychologist (most are not). In addition, screening environments are usually highly structured, and upsetting the routine will be of little benefit to your child. Remember that the main purpose is to determine whether he or she is developmentally delayed in any way; if it turns out that this is not the case, consider your mission accomplished.

"And then he said... and he's really good in... but he's even BETTER at..."

2. DO watch to make sure that the behaviors your child exhibits are interpreted correctly. While the majority of parents of high-potential children report that preschool screening was a positive experience, some come away from it confused, frustrated, or furious. Very bright and creative children can be especially unpredictable in this kind of situation. If the observer has been encouraged to view any and all deviations from the norm as deficiencies, he or she may misinterpret the reactions that are common to such children.

One mother observed as the examiner held up a finger and asked her son, "What is this?" The child replied, "A digit." Because digit was not listed on the answer form as a correct response, the examiner marked the item incorrect. Later the examiner asked the child, "A red stoplight says stop. What does a green stoplight say?" The literal four-year-old replied, "Stoplights don't say anything. They don't talk at all." The examiner marked the answer sheet, "Child does not respond." To top it off, the boy had slightly below-average motor skills. The final report indicated that he was at risk for school problems due to developmental delays.

In reality, the boy may well have been at risk, but certainly not due to developmental delays. Any potential problems stemmed from advanced thinking patterns coupled with slightly low but still acceptable motor skills. The mother's immediate concern was that school personnel were ready to enroll her son in a "remedial life skills" class which he almost certainly would have found repetitive and boring. All that saved him from a negative introduction to school was his mother's tactful but tenacious insistence that the screening scores be evaluated in light of other data.

3. KEEP an open mind. Even if you are confident that your child is gifted, don't ignore any evidence the screening may reveal that he or she does, in fact, merit a closer look. Remember that the whole purpose of preschool screening is to discover possible problems early, before they have the chance to impact a child's school performance. The best approach for you to take is to pay attention and keep an open mind. If the examiner thinks that your child needs more observation, go ahead and get some. Choose someone you trust — *and someone who has at least a rudimentary knowledge of the needs of high-ability children* — to deliver the second opinion.

In time, the slow but steady rise in interest among educators and parents regarding the needs of promising children may effect some changes in the whole preschool screening process. Until then, about all you can do is take it for what it is: one way, but certainly not the *only* way, to learn more about your child.

CHAPTER 10

The Early Entrance
Dilemma

Early school entrance is one of the most hotly debated issues in the field of gifted education. Proponents argue that gifted children who wait until they are the "right" chronological age to start school are at risk for boredom and the host of learning, behavior, and discipline problems that may ensue. They also maintain that children who don't use their ability in early years may lose some of it. Opponents worry that children who start school at a younger age than their classmates may have difficulties due to "immaturity." Many of them subscribe to the "early ripe, early rot" theory that children who "rush" natural timetables will burn out more quickly than others.

As in any good debate, there is some truth on both sides, and the irony is that most educators admit it. Almost without exception, educational theorists (and many teachers as well) agree that the decision to put every American child in school the first September after he or she reaches age five is a purely arbitrary one that takes no notice of individual differences. In reality, one child may be ready at four and a half, another at five, and still another at six or even seven. Plus children who do start at the "same" age may actually have up to eleven months' difference between them — 20 percent of a kindergartner's entire life experience.

In the face of these known discrepancies, public schools (and most private ones) still blithely proceed as if school readiness were an either/or issue instead of a continuum. The vast majority of American children march off to school when the calendar says they must. It's a fact you're probably going to have to deal with, like it or not.

This doesn't mean that you're entirely without options, however. But you will have to take responsibility for determining the point at which you feel your child should begin formal schooling. And once you've made that determination, you will have to convince school officials that you're right. Chances are you'll have to go it alone, with whatever help you can glean from preschool screening.

The goal, of course, is to achieve the optimal "fit" between your child and the school program, both now and in the future. You're not likely to have much luck changing either your child or the school system to facilitate this fit, so your best shot at success lies in having the child and the system cross paths when the child's needs and the program's characteristics are at closest proximity. A prediction of when this will happen can never be better than a guess, but if you do your homework you stand a chance of getting the two together at a time that's right for both.

Essentially, you have three choices: You may try to put your child in school before your district's cutoff date; you may enter him or her "on time;"or you may wait a year and have your child start later than other children. As we'll see shortly, each option has its advantages and disadvantages.

Prior to making any choice, you must closely examine two important variables: your child and the school. Many parents make the mistake of focusing *only* on the former. They assume that all schools have the same requirements for success at the kindergarten and first-grade levels. Parents of gifted children also often assume that the goals of these programs are strictly academic — in other words, that they emphasize reading, writing, math, and subject area mastery. While this is the case for *some* programs, it is definitely not for all or even most.

Here is where parents and school officials usually have their first big misunderstanding. Parents emerge from their initial conference appalled that "the kid reads at a fourth-grade level, and they won't let him in kindergarten because he can't cut a straight line!" Educators head for the faculty lounge muttering that "sure the kid can read, but he doesn't have any social or motor skills!"

Who's right? Both, or neither — it depends. If the kindergarten or first-grade program is a very traditional, old-fashioned one that stresses social skills and sensory experiences, then a parent with an academically precocious child who is slightly delayed in social and motor skills is missing the point if he or she demands early entrance. The child may not be ready for what the school has to offer.

To further complicate this issue, the last decade has seen significant shifts in kindergarten and first-grade education, and the way readiness is assessed has not always kept up. Many primary programs today are highly academic in nature. A great deal of time is spent in formal study of pre-reading and math activities and other structured study of subject matter. Yet in many districts the readiness requirements continue to be based on the kindergartens of ten years ago.

For example, an early entrance screening may require a child to draw recognizable geometric figures, cut out shapes to within one-half inch of their contours, skip and hop, and color inside the lines. It may not even touch upon the mastery of reading or math skills or the child's fund of knowledge, despite the fact that these are precisely the skills emphasized by the program.

In other words, the child who can read fluently but isn't good with scissors may be asked to mark time for another year, until he or she can cut well enough to spend most of the day in reading activities far below his or her level of functioning.... Of course it's illogical, and this time the illogic is on the part of the system.

What to do? Start by determining whether the activities your child is advanced in are those on which the program will be focusing. Spend a half-day observing a class. Talk to teachers. Ask for a description of the curriculum, and sample worksheets if they are available. If a large part of the day is spent on pre-reading activities and your child can already read, then you have cause for concern. The same holds true if a large part of the day is spent on fine motor practice and your child has been designing and sewing doll clothes for years. In either case there's a distinct possibility that your child will be bored with the program as it is, and waiting another year will only make matters worse.

On the other hand, if the areas your child has mastered are not covered extensively, then many of the school experiences will be new to him or her. Knowing this, you can begin deciding which of three possible Septembers will offer your child the best chance at both success and stimulation.

Let's consider the pros and cons of each.

Early Entrance

You should consider early entrance for your child *if*:

🐿 He or she is at a level of achievement where the program can provide challenging material without making special provisions, and

🐿 He or she has the social and motor skills necessary for success in these areas.

Your child doesn't have to be outstanding in *all* areas. But he or she should be at a point where successful growth is possible.

Provided that your child fits this picture, you can expect (or, more realistically, hope) to realize these advantages from early entrance:

🐿 Your child will be less likely to be bored with school.

🐿 Your child will be able to complete public schooling and get on with career preparation at an earlier age.

This latter point can prove significant if he or she ultimately decides to pursue something like an M.D. or a degree in applied physics, which may entail years of graduate work.

☞ Your child will have the opportunity to associate with others who are at a similarly advanced level of thinking.

"If I sold teddy I could send the money to starving people."

And I could sell my tricycle!

☞ Your child will be challenged to apply himself or herself.

Children who breeze through the first few years of school don't need to apply themselves and miss important lessons in learning how. ("Why work hard if everything is easy?") This may lead to underachievement in the future.

But there's a dark side to this picture. Even the child who seems perfectly suited for early entrance may have problems because of it, then and later. Here are a few of the disadvantages:

🔧 The more precocious the child, the less likely this option will help to any significant degree.

A four-year-old who reads at a fifth-grade level is always going to have difficulty with inappropriate reading instruction, regardless of when he or she starts school.

🔧 Your child may be "under a microscope" for the first months or even years.

This probably won't happen in an enlightened school system. But if early entrance is approved only after vocal disagreements with school personnel, your child may pay the price. All of his or her future behaviors may be examined in light of the early entrance.

Your child will always be younger than his or her classmates.

This may not seem particularly worrisome during the primary school years, but what about high school? What about the year when everyone else gets a driver's license? Starts dating? Is tempted to experiment with drugs or alcohol? What are your child's chances of coping at fourteen with issues that his or her fifteen-year-old friends are facing? During adolescence, every second of maturity counts.

"On-Time" Entrance

Your second option is to let policy take its course and enroll your child in school according to the standard guidelines operating in your area. One obvious reason for making this choice is if your child is very bright but doesn't yet know the material to be covered. He or she will probably find the introduction to certain areas new and stimulating, and the problem will lie not with the nature of the work but with the time spent developing each skill. Your child may enjoy going over something the first time but start losing interest the second or third. Still, if much of the original material is fresh, then standard placement is appropriate and you can try to get the teacher to provide enrichment and extension activities.

Another reason to consider on-time entrance is if your child's talent is not addressed by the school to any great degree. A child who is brilliant in music will not have to suffer through hours of inappropriate instruction, as the child who is gifted in math most certainly will.

Increasingly, there is a third reason to follow the traditional timetable: the availability of special programming for gifted children. More and more districts are offering this as early as kindergarten and first grade. If you're fortunate enough to have access to such programming, you can probably assume that it was designed to meet the needs of bright children who enter school with their age peers.

Here are the advantages of on-time entrance:

It's easy.

All you have to do is follow the instructions the school district sends you, and voila! Your child is enrolled in school. Importantly, this happens without subjecting the child to undue scrutiny. As a result, he or she is more likely to be evaluated according to his or her own behavior, rather than yours at enrollment time.

It lessens the danger that your child will develop negative attitudes toward school at a later age.

Some researchers say that early entrance leads to such attitudes. It's worth keeping in mind.

Your child will reach certain developmental milestones (puberty, legal drinking and driving ages) at roughly the same time as his or her classmates do.

A year seems like forever to the teen who can't yet get a driver's license — and to the child whose body is still childlike at a time when everyone else's is noticeably changing.

There are two major disadvantages to on-time entrance for your gifted child:

It virtually assures boredom at various steps along the way. Although this can be minimized with the help of sympathetic and well-trained teachers, the exceptionally intelligent child will always be ahead of his or her peers.

He or she will not be challenged by the school experience.

By the time truly challenging work does surface, the child may be seriously behind in study skills and the ability to apply himself or herself.

Delayed Entrance

Waiting another year before starting school can have distinct payoffs for the thoughtful family who goes into it with a well-formed plan. Parents who choose this option do so primarily out of the belief that the school system doesn't have all that much to offer their children in the first place, so the longer they can post-pone it, the better. Some parents feel that another year of "home schooling" would be more enriching; others take this opportunity to find an advanced preschool that offers greater stimulation than the traditional kindergarten approach.

More and more educational theorists argue that formal schooling should not begin until age seven or eight. Here are the advantages you can expect to realize from late entrance:

☞ Your child's learning potential may increase because of the extra time spent in wide-ranging exploratory learning experiences (in the home and/or preschool) rather than the more structured school setting.

Some parents believe in giving their child as much of this as possible during the early years and accelerating later — for example, by skipping from fifth to seventh grade. They feel that acceleration is an option better exercised later, when the choices have become more limited.

☞ Your child may be better equipped to handle the stress and strain of boredom.

Since even early entrance can't alleviate this problem entirely, it may be better to enroll the child when he or she is more mature and capable of dealing with it. The older child may be more likely to be able to draw on his or her own resources to fill "extra" time — and to do so in a way that will not aggravate teachers.

Delayed entrance is also appropriate for the child suffering from severe *dysynchrony* — a gap between intellectual development and other areas of growth. Children who are physically immature and whose emotional development does not permit them to handle stress well are already struggling to reconcile their intellect with what they see as their "shortcomings." It doesn't help to have these underscored by daily self-comparison to other children.

If your child is dysynchronous, the best approach may be de-layed entrance combined with the advocacy strategies outlined on pages 185-205.

Here are some possible disadvantages of delayed entrance:

♪ Your child could end up being the biggest kid in class (which may be more of a problem for girls than boys). If your child already feels different because of advanced intellect, this will only widen the gap between your child and his or her peers.

🔔 Your child may be more emotionally mature and may find his or her classmates to be unbearably silly or babyish.

🔔 Your motives for delayed entrance may be questioned. People may assume you want your child to be the biggest, brightest, and best in class.

□ ■ □

Whatever you decide to do about enrolling your child in school, keep in mind that hindsight is always 20/20. No matter what choice you make, your child's school career will include both successes and disappointments. Some may be the direct result of decisions you made on his or her behalf; the rest probably would have occurred anyway.

About the only advice we can give is to investigate your options thoroughly and weigh your choices carefully. Then do what your own parents did: Take the credit for the things that go right, and assume that the things that don't were beyond your control.

CHAPTER 11

How to Be
Your Child's Advocate
in the School System

The day a child sets off for school — be it preschool, daycare, or kindergarten — is often a tough one for parents. It signals the dawn of a new era, and it's both exciting and anxiety-producing.

The anxiety stems in part from the fact that everyone must take on new roles. Your child must learn to be a kindergartener or a daycare kid as well as a son or daughter. You must learn to share the care of your child with a group of strangers — and to be your child's advocate in the system. This may mean supporting the system in what it's doing well. Or it may require you to call the attention of school personnel to how they might better meet the special needs of your child.

Too many parents wait to get involved in the school setting until a crisis arises, at which point they charge in like gangbusters. A far better approach is to forge a partnership with your child's other educators from the start. It's not only more fair to help create the good times; it's also more effective. Like the rest of us, teachers and administrators prefer to work in a nonthreatening and supportive atmosphere. While both truth and right may be on your side when you pick up the phone to shout, "I'm a tax-paying parent, and I demand to be heard!", this technique is known to have a negative impact on the limbic systems of teachers.

This is not to say that you must accept any and all decisions that educators make about your child. He or she is *your* child, and you *are* paying taxes (or tuition). You have both a legal right and a moral obligation to exercise your say. There will be times when your child will provoke the system, and you will need to cooperate with it to find out how to make things better. And there will be times when the system will mightily provoke you and your child, and you will need to advocate on your own behalf.

There are two kinds of effective advocacy: *proactive* and *reactive*. In proactive advocacy, you try to anticipate needs and prevent problems in advance. In reactive advocacy, you respond to a problem.

Proactive Advocacy

There are several ways to go about proactively advocating for a positive educational setting for your child. The first of these has already been discussed: finding the right school or program. While this won't necessarily eliminate conflict, it should help keep it to a minimum.

This may not be an option when your child reaches kindergarten or first grade. Public schools frequently offer only one educational approach. Even if different schools in your district espouse different philosophies, where your child goes may depend more on where you live than on his or her educational needs.

Many schools today offer programs for high-potential and gifted students. If your child's school is one that does, you will need to find out whether your child qualifies and whether it seems likely that he or she will benefit from it. Although these two considerations are often seen as synonymous, they are not.

Gifted programs are still relatively rare at the kindergarten and first-grade levels, one reason being that it is difficult to identify appropriate children for them. The more factors that can be considered when placing children in gifted programs, the more accurate the placement. In the upper grades this usually means looking at teacher recommendations, student products, and standardized test scores. For children new to the system, these data are seldom available. Schools must rely on input from parents and on individualized I.Q. scores.

If you know that your child's school has some sort of special programming for high-ability youngsters, find out who it is designed to serve and ask if there is a parent referral form. (It may look something like the checklists found on pages 7-12.) Once you complete and return the form, if it appears from your remarks on it that your child might benefit from special programming, you may be asked to give your permission for further testing. Before agreeing to this, be sure to ask what tests will be given, who will be administering them, and how the results will be used. Also ask how the results will correlate with the objectives of the program. If the special class being offered is one in Suzuki violin and the entrance qualifier is an I.Q. score, you should question the validity of both the identification procedures and the program philosophy.

If it seems that the stated objectives of the program and your child's needs would be a good match, the next step is to determine the quality of the classes. While most programs for the gifted are everything they should be, some are not. The following questions can help you to make a reasonably thorough evaluation.

☐   Is the identification process appropriate for the stated goals of the class? That is, are students with math ability placed in math-related activities, or are all children with special abilities routinely lumped together?

☐   Is the identification process multidimensional?

☐   Do the teachers have training in the special needs of the gifted?

☐   Is parental involvement in the program encouraged?

☐   Are gifted students given an opportunity to interact with intellectual peers?

☐   Are gifted students mainstreamed for at least a part of their day?

☐   What is the attitude of teachers, aids, and administrators toward gifted children?

☐   How much of the activity is teacher-directed, and how much is student-directed under teacher guidance?

☐   What proportion of the activities encourage creative expression?

☐   Is creative problem-solving a component of the program? Do problem-solving activities allow for many possible answers and a lot of exploration?

☐   What is the student/teacher ratio?

☐   What are the opportunities for independent study?

☐   Are the teachers particularly well-versed in the material being presented?

☐   Is the program flexible?

☐   Are the standards for the program high, and are they clearly expressed to all parties concerned?

☐   How much money is available for the program?

☐   What is the atmosphere in the work areas? Do teachers and students seem stimulated by what they are doing? Do they display a mutual respect?

☐   What are the priorities of the program's administrators?

☐   Does the district have a "ceilings on" or "ceilings off" approach to subject mastery?

A ceiling on a particular subject means that instruction in that area may not advance beyond that point for any student or group of students. For example, students who have mastered all the second-grade math curriculum may engage in horizontal enrichment in math but may not begin work on the third-grade curriculum. With a ceilings-off approach, the students may progress through the materials at whatever pace is appropriate for mastery, regardless of grade level. Ceilings-on is often equated with enrichment; ceilings-off, with acceleration.

☐   How is the communication from one grade level to the next? From one subject area to the next?

☐   Are counseling services provided?

Even if there are no special programs at your child's level, you are not entirely without options. You may request that your child be placed with a particular teacher. In some districts this is a matter of routine; in others it is accepted but not encouraged; in still others it is not possible. You won't know until you ask.

Plan ahead and proceed carefully. Start by having it very clear in your mind why you feel your child needs a certain kind of instructional atmosphere. Consider both your child's ability level and his or her personality. Next, talk to the principal. State your reasons for concern and seek his or her assistance in scheduling times when you can watch all of the teachers at that grade level in action. In later years you will probably know which teachers you prefer for your child, but as you come into the system you will want to make more formal observations.

You should initiate this process as early as January of the year preceding your child's enrollment. Many administrators make tentative staffing decisions at that point, and your request, combined with those of other parents, may affect those decisions. *Phrase your request carefully.* In no way should you imply anything negative about individual teachers or indicate that your concern is based on stories you have heard about this or that one's behavior. Instead, take a neutral yet positive approach. Suggest by your cheerful but assertive manner that of course you're all interested in what's best for children, and you're there to do your part. Be candid if you feel that your child is at risk for boredom or disillusionment because he or she is advanced in a particular area, but don't overdo the stories of his or her remarkable feats.

It is very likely that the people you talk to will try to accommodate you. There is always the possibility, however, that your first contact will be with someone who does not accept that giftedness is cause for concern, and will therefore be predisposed to view you as a pushy parent. Until you know what you are dealing with, assume the best and be prepared for the worst. In this way you can avoid two common pitfalls to successful advocacy: patronizing those who might have supported you, and antagonizing those who might have left you alone.

What should you look for in your child's teacher? Try to find as many of these characteristics as you can — but don't expect to find all of them:

- ☐ Is in good health and has lots of energy
- ☐ Exhibits and appreciates creativity and originality
- ☐ Has a sense of humor
- ☐ Is firm but flexible
- ☐ Has a tolerance for ambiguity
- ☐ Really enjoys young children
- ☐ Focuses on what children can do rather than what they can't do
- ☐ Is receptive to new ideas
- ☐ Displays intellectual curiosity
- ☐ Is knowledgeable about and experienced in both the theories and practice of early childhood development
- ☐ Is observant of children's behavior
- ☐ Is clear about his or her own philosophy of education
- ☐ Is patient
- ☐ Is open to suggestions

Another more general strategy for proactive advocacy is to establish early a true spirit of teamwork with the personnel at your child's school. If you're later disappointed with the quality of the education being offered, your opinions will stand a better chance of being heard if you've already established rapport with the powers that be.

A good forum for discussion is the parent/teacher conference. All schools routinely schedule these, usually two or three times a year. The more prepared you are, the more will be accomplished. Some suggestions:

• **Be ready to voice some specific thoughts on what you have liked about your child's experience to date.**
Let the teacher know that you appreciate her care with bulletin boards, or the ordered way in which her class travels to the gym, and she'll find it that much easier to hear you out on other matters.

• **Bring some descriptions of what your child likes to do in his or her non-school hours.**
The teacher may never know of your child's driving passion for ballet, karate, or growing begonias unless you alert him.

• **Be ready to ask specific questions.**
What's the daily schedule for the class? How does the teacher feel about ability grouping? What areas of the curriculum does the district emphasize? What subjects does the teacher most enjoy teaching?

• **If possible, offer to volunteer in some capacity.**
Volunteers enjoy several advantages over non-volunteer parents. They have the satisfaction of knowing that they add to the educational environment of the school, they have a closer relationship with staff, and they are on the spot to see what's really going on.

• **Finally, come prepared to listen.**
The teacher's answers to your questions will help you to find a common ground — one from which you can both support her activities and negotiate specific issues. Leave time as well for the teacher to ask questions of you and share her concerns.

When you do your best to get along with your child's teacher, you are not abdicating your future rights to challenge the system.

In fact, you're improving your chances of being heard later, should the need arise. By the end of a polite and mutually informative conference, you'll probably have a pretty good idea as to whether the two of you are on the same wavelength. If you are, terrific. If you aren't, then at least you will have determined where your differences lie without antagonizing anyone, and you can proceed accordingly.

Reactive Advocacy

What if you've done everything you can to form positive relationships with school personnel and things still aren't working out to your satisfaction? This is where reactive advocacy strategies enter in.

The first rule of reactive advocacy is that early intervention is better than late. While it's counterproductive to run to the school at every complaint your child voices, serious concerns require serious attention. A child who is bored and/or unhappy in the early school years is at risk for problems later.

How can you tell if the situation is serious enough to merit attention? What seems like the most obvious clue — your child telling you so — isn't always foolproof.

For example, six-year-old Franklin came home one day and announced that math class "made him tired." Because he was a bright child in many ways, his father naturally assumed that Franklin's boredom was the result of already knowing the material. Armed with stories from other parents of gifted children about recalcitrant school systems, Franklin's father firmly requested that his son be moved to a more challenging math class. This was done, and Franklin's attitude toward math deteriorated even further. Ultimately, after much achievement testing, it was determined that Franklin didn't know the material that was being covered in either class — he was simply not interested in math.

Young children are prone to sweeping and often vague remarks about what happens during the day. You know that this is true for other areas of their lives, so why not school? It's best to closely examine any such comment before taking action. Franklin really did have a problem, but not the one it was first assumed to be; another child's case might have a different outcome.

If your child is complaining of boredom or having to do "baby work,"request a mastery test. Most teachers have them on hand for particular skills. If a child proves that he has mastered certain materials, he or she should not be asked to repeat them. If it turns out that the child has mastered the lion's share, he or she should be asked only to work on the remaining ones. And if the child has *not* mastered the materials, everyone should retire gracefully from the fray and help the child to learn them in a way that he or she finds at least marginally appealing.

It's important to distinguish between *appropriate* and *inappropriate* boredom. Appropriate boredom occurs when a child is not interested in learning a particular skill but ought to anyway. Multiplication tables may be "boring," but if the teacher has made some effort to present them in an appealing fashion, then the child has been met halfway and should get on with the job. Inappropriate boredom occurs when a child already knows the material. Under these circumstances, the parents have every right to insist that adjustments be made.

Recognizing and Responding to Early Childhood Stress

Often our children won't even tell us as much as Franklin told his father. They'll describe school as "fine" or "okay" and airily dismiss our attempts at probing questions. If you have cause to suspect that your child's one-word answers aren't revealing the whole story, there are signs of stress you can look for.

Keep in mind, however, that radical shifts in personality are considered normal for some children in the early developmental stages. If your child exhibits a number of the characteristics described below, you may have cause for concern, or your child may just be "going through a phase." Does your child have a history of struggling to adjust to new situations? Then perhaps it's best to offer lots of unconditional love and work on coping strategies. Or has your child always adjusted to life fairly easily, but is suddenly showing abrupt behavior changes? Then you should take action.

Following are some recognized indicators of stress in young children:

Any change in sleeping patterns, including waking up in the middle of the night, nightmares or general night terrors, or a sudden desire to sleep much of the time. Infants are known to use the technique of falling asleep to shut out overwhelming stimuli; occasionally an older child will react to emotional exhaustion in a similar manner.

Any change in eating habits, including eating very little or much more than usual.

Any change in toileting habits, perhaps coupled with reversion to "baby" behaviors that were let go years earlier. Some children react to a new experience in this way because they feel nostalgic for what they perceive to have been easier times. Others subconsciously hope that a "baby" won't be welcome in school, and if they act like one they won't have to go.

"Perfect" behavior in the school setting, coupled with wildly erratic behavior at home. Some children store their pent-up frustration all day and let it out at home, where they feel safe. Wildly erratic behavior should not be confused with the normal exuberance of children who need exercise after sitting for much of the day.

Pronounced avoidance behavior. Some children marshal extraordinary resources to avoid a situation they find painful. One kindergartner always managed to be out of sight whenever her bus rounded the corner in the morning — searching for an "injured" kitten behind the garage or burrowing under a bush for a "lost" library book were just two of her excuses.

General crankiness, weepiness, or diminished ability to roll with the punches. Children who formerly took small frustrations and setbacks in stride may suddenly be upset by every little thing. If they're using all of their coping resources to function in an environment they find difficult, they may have none left over for zippers that won't zip and peas that roll off the fork.

Total lack of interest in an activity that was previously a passion. This should not be confused with a normal and gradual shift in interests. What it represents is a denial of the child's sense of self.

Five-year-old Penny was a highly creative artist who loved to paint until she started school. By October she was referring to her paint set as "dumb" and refusing to paint, draw, or color. As it turned out, her kindergarten teacher valued "staying in the lines" over creative endeavor and was philosophically opposed to painting suns any color but yellow. When Penny was unable to be true to herself and to the requirements of her school, she gave the whole thing up as a bad job.

" I have a headache in my stomach ! "

Complaints of illness that do not have a specific physical origin. While an occasional headache or stomach ache is nothing to worry about, a child who repeatedly complains of "hurting" or being sick may indeed be having a stress reaction.

Gerry started first grade as a reasonably healthy child. By Christmas he was refusing every weekday breakfast on the grounds that his tummy hurt. His pediatrician diagnosed him as having a stress-related spastic colon. It didn't bother him much on weekends or during the summer, and the symptoms lessened when he moved from an exceptionally rigid first-grade class to a more gentle and flexible second-grade environment.

Describing oneself in negative terms. All children experiment with various insults in the early years to see how others will react to them. A child who starts regularly referring to himself or herself as "stupid" or "dumb" could be in trouble, however. This may indicate that the child perceives that he or she is not of value in the school setting.

Six-year-old Zachary's mother noticed the change within the first few weeks of his starting first grade. A normally ebullient child who didn't hesitate to tell others about all the things he was good at, he seldom mentioned how he was doing in school. When she questioned him, he replied, "Do we *have* to talk about that?" Finally she took a different approach. "How do you *feel* when you're in school?" she asked. Silence. "It's okay to tell me," Mom urged. "I want to know if you feel good, or bad, or happy, or sad." Then Zachary answered, "I feel *naughty.*" To Mom, that signaled the need for action.

What should you do if your child evidences some of these signs of early childhood stress? *Don't panic.* If the behaviors you observe are not overly pronounced, there is probably no need for serious worry. Young children go through periods of equilibrium and disequilibrium. Disequilibrium is a necessary stage of dissatisfaction which moves a child from one set of skills to the next. Some children proceed smoothly through these transitions; for others they're a struggle. Resist the urge to overreact, watch for further developments, and use the coping strategies that have worked for your family before.

Meanwhile, try to make the rest of your child's life as conflict-free as possible. Although it's hard to avoid a fight with a five-year-old intent on mayhem, it may be worth relaxing some of the less important rules for a while. Stick to the essential principles of behavior, but backtrack a bit in terms of your child's personal responsibilities. Given the other issues he or she is dealing with, it's no big deal to go back to zipping your child's coat or walking your child to the bus stop in the morning.

It's also helpful to affirm the feelings you perceive your child to be having. It is *not* appropriate to say, "Mommy knows you're miserable. Mommy wishes you didn't have to go to that mean old school either." It is perfectly all right to say, "You seem angry a lot lately. I'll bet it's hard to behave all morning in school and then try to follow rules at home, too. But I can't let you keep kicking the dog. Would you like to take out your drum and make some really angry noise?"

If the headaches, bedwetting, or nightmares persist, or if they are very pronounced and atypical of your child's behavior, then it's time for more specific advocacy. Your first step should be to talk with a child development professional, perhaps your pediatrician. Someone with experience in this area can help you to discover whether your child's reaction to school is *internally* or *externally* motivated. Each requires different coping strategies and intervention techniques. The internal drives common to gifted children were discussed in Chapter 2, so we will now look more closely at some of the outside influences that can result in early childhood stress.

Externally caused stress in children can be a result of adults having inappropriate expectations of them. These can be as obvious as expecting three-year-olds to sit quietly for extended periods of time, or as subtle as implying to a five-year-old who reads fluently that she should be happy to spend hours every week drawing lines from A's to apples and from B's to balls.

In checking your child's life for inappropriate expectations, start by looking at home — as painful as this might be. Examine the attitudes of parents and siblings toward the child who is having trouble. Are you all implying that the child is not all he or she could be? Are you focusing on what your child can do rather than on who he or she is? If so, it's better to find out now than in ten years, when your 15-year-old is coping with stress by developing ulcers, experimenting with drugs, or dropping out of school.

It is not our intent to make parents of high-ability children feel guilty; most of us do well enough at that already. Nevertheless, it pays to scrutinize our own behaviors on occasion. We all want our gifted children to be successful; we want to be proud of them; we're accustomed to their mastering many skills quickly and seeming to be older than their years. Thus it's easy to overreact when they stumble or fall. But because they're still young and can't always articulate their problems, it's up to us to be alert to times when we must advocate on their behalf — not only in their relationships with teachers, but also in their relationships with *us*.

Each of us has had moments as parents we wish we could live over. We've yelled at our children when they didn't deserve it. We've sent them to their rooms for minor offenses. We've vented on them our righteous indignation over relatively petty things — misbehaving at parties, arguing with siblings, pulling the cat's tail, spilling their milk. We don't like it when they disobey. We don't like it when they embarrass us. *But mostly we don't like it when they fail to meet our expectations.* And because we know what they're capable of — we've seen their I.Q. scores; we've watched them leap ahead of their age peers in so many ways — our expectations are very high indeed. And often these are tied to our own needs for validation that we're doing a good job as parents. Even the best-intentioned of us can confuse our own needs with those of our children.

Are your expectations for your child reasonable, or too high? Find out by answering the following questions with *always, sometimes,* or *never.*

1. *I believe that it's my responsibility to set the highest standards for my child.*

2. *I worry about what my friends and relatives will think if my child doesn't perform well in school.*

3. *I get more upset when my child makes a mistake in public than when he or she does so in private.*

4. *When I think my child can do better at something, I say so.*

5. *I believe that my child can do* **anything** *he or she wants to do.*

6. *I lose patience when I try to explain something to my child and he or she just doesn't get it.*

7. *I lose patience when my child takes a long time to do something.*

8. *I'm disappointed when my child turns in an average performance.*

9. *I reprimand my child for being lazy or silly.*

10. *When my child does something, I expect him or her to keep trying until he or she gets it right.*

The more times you answered ***always,*** the greater the need for you to back off! Too often, kids interpret high expectations as implying that they're not good enough. Over time, this turns into the belief that they're not good, period.

When we have expectations for our children, we're letting them know that every individual must grow emotionally, socially, and intellectually. When we overdo it, however, we're putting our children at risk for self-esteem problems both now and in the future. What we're saying is, "I expect you *always* to do your best, in *everything,* all the time!" Nobody can take that much pressure for long. (Could you?)

One mother remembers having to rein in her own too-high expectations: "When I looked at Sarah, I kept thinking of what she could be someday. I saw what she already was — the brightest kid in her class, a budding musician, a kid who could read at age three. I'd get so impatient when she did less than what I expected of her. And then I'd remember: *she's just a little girl.*"

Recommended Reading

The Stress-Proof Child: A Loving Parent's Guide by Antoinette Saunders and Bonnie Remsberg. (New York: Holt, Rinehart and Winston, 1984).

This is a down-to-earth book that helps parents to recognize signs of stress in children and offers appropriate strategies for helping a stressed child as well as ideas for "stress-proofing" your kids. It focuses on elementary-age children, but with some creative reading (and application) it should also be of assistance even in preschool years.

□ ■ □

What if your child is exhibiting signs of stress that are clearly related not to the home but to the school? There are ways to determine the source of the problem.

Start by gathering information — by observing and listening to your child as unobtrusively as possible.

🐾 **Provide opportunities for dramatic play, and be alert to clues about what goes on in school.** One mother discovered the degree of conformity required in her first-grader's classroom when she walked in on a group of neighborhood children playing school. As they scribbled on the chalkboard and cut up piece of paper, their conversation was peppered with comments like, "Careful, that's not right" and "Can't you follow directions?" A child who looked up and caught sight of her shouted, "I wasn't doing nothing!" and burst into tears.

🐾 **Listen to how your child plays when acting out roles or using superhero figures, robots, or little plastic people.** If you're capable of a little subtlety, you might even join in or initiate a play session. The characters can pretend to be riding to school, lining up for lunch, or beginning a reading class. Resist the temptation to lead the little plastic witnesses.

🐾 **Avoid asking leading questions.** It's tricky to get information out of young children in such a way that your obvious concern does not color their responses. A parent who asks a child, "Who did you play with today?" and receives the answer, "Nobody," might feel a prick of worry about the child's social life. If the next question is, "Does that make you feel lonely?", the answer will probably be "Yes." Phrased differently, the questions might yield different responses. Try: "Tell me some things you did by yourself today," followed by "And what kinds of things did you do with your friends?"

🐾 **Provide plenty of art materials and ask open-ended questions about the results.** "Tell me about this picture of a girl sitting at her desk.... You say she's stabbing her pencil into the paper? I wonder why she's doing that. What do you think?"

Do some abstract finger-painting or watercolor yourself, commenting as you go. "I'm going to paint how I feel when I bake bread, all sunny yellow and smooth like this.... Now I'm going to paint how I felt this morning when that truck driver honked and yelled at me. Pass the red and black." Restrict your involvement to modeling and general comments. There's no point in trying to determine why a child is feeling pressured by putting further pressure on him or her.

One mother-daughter team glued circles on popsicle sticks, then drew happy faces on one side and sad faces on the other. They added hair and little outfits, and over a period of weeks the characters developed names and personalities. Mostly they were used for free play, but once they came in handy when Mom said, "Now Flouncy is going to get her snack because it is snack time. She is trying to decide where to sit. I wonder how she feels?" Her three-year-old, who never said a word about nursery school, turned Flouncy's face to sad.

With a bit more creativity, Mom was able to determine that while most of the school morning was okay for her daughter, snack time was a strain. This particular nursery school promoted self-reliance by having the children carry their own juice in breakable glasses, and the little girl was terrified of dropping hers. When Mom shared this information with the director, she was told, "This is part of the curriculum. No exceptions or adjustments will be made." Further investigation led to the discovery of many similar rules, and thanks to Flouncy the three-year-old soon moved to another setting.

☁ **Pay close attention to papers and other work your child brings home.** If you see a pattern of confusion developing — in other words, if neither you nor your child can figure out why the teacher makes the kinds of marks he or she does — ask for clarification. This doesn't mean that you should run for the phone every time an item is marked wrong. Mistakes are acceptable, and dealing with them builds character. Ongoing confusion merits looking into, however, since it usually reflects confusion about expectations.

Four-year-old Philip repeatedly came home from nursery school with a completed worksheet and an identical blank sheet. All the other kids were getting happy faces on their first attempts, he said, but he would have to do his over again if he wanted a happy face. He was confused, as were his parents, because it appeared that Philip's responses were correct.

The children were supposed to circle the beginning sounds of certain words as the teacher said them. According to Philip's reports of which words the teacher spoke (he had an exceptional memory and usually reported accurately), he was indicating the correct responses.

A conference with the teacher revealed that his answers were indeed *correct,* but not *acceptable.* The directions said to *circle* the letter, and Philip, a very creative child who already knew how to read, had drawn a pumpkin around the P, a house around the H, and a cloud around the C.

☁ **Use bibliotherapy to help your child share his or her feelings about uncomfortable situations.** (For an explanation of bibliotherapy, see page 81.) You may want to read together some of the books in the "Troubled Times" category on page 84 and see what responses they elicit.

Once you have gathered all the information you can at home, head for the school. This is where your initial efforts to establish rapport with the staff will come in handy.

Make your first appointment with your child's teacher or teaching team. It's tempting when you're upset with a particular classroom situation to go directly to an administrator, and ultimately you may have to take that step. But most teachers find it very threatening to be talked about before they know that something is wrong, and there is no need to put anyone on the defensive at this point. Besides, the purpose of this visit is to find out all you can about events in the classroom, and nobody knows those better than the individuals who work directly with your child.

Begin by explaining to the teacher that your child is having a tough time adjusting and you want to help. Ask him or her to describe your child to you. Ask for specific descriptions of the child's behavior and attitude in the areas you feel might be trouble spots. Then ask the teacher how he or she arrived at those descriptions.

If your child has complained of repetitive math work and the teacher describes him or her as "coming along nicely," find out how the teacher made this determination. Was a pre-test given? Is it possible for you to see the math curriculum? How long does it take your child to finish his or her work, in comparison to the other children? What activities are provided for those who finish early? Are these activities more of the same, or are they substantially different? How are children encouraged to participate in them?

Listen to the words the teacher uses to describe your child's behavior. Similar personality characteristics can be perceived in very different ways, depending on the eye and the mindset of the beholder. Compare the attitudes implicit on both sides of the following "equations":

energetic = hyperactive

humorous, witty = flip, glib

talkative = mouthy

consistent = rigid, stubborn

adaptable, flexible = inconsistent

trustful, open = gullible

calm = dull

introspective = moody, brooding

reserved = inhibited, secretive

enthusiastic = impulsive, overeager

Does your child have attributes which you view as positive but the teacher seems not to approve of or appreciate?

Wind up this conference by telling the teacher what you plan to do next. Explain that you need time to process what you have learned, and that you will call him or her when you have decided how to proceed. A teacher who is left uninformed will be anxious, and this may lead to further classroom problems for your child.

Set the tone for your next meeting by trying to find some mutual ground. It's appropriate to note that the teacher has many children to be concerned about, and to express your appreciation that he or she was willing to share information with you.

Afterward, get clear in your mind what you perceive the problem or problems to be. Is it social, emotional, academic, or a combination? What expectations do school personnel have for your child that you feel are inappropriate? What expectations do you feel are appropriate? For each problem area, try to determine at least one way in which you and your child can work together toward a solution. Then come up with a change or changes regarding the problem area that you would like the school to make. Finally, turn your list of concerns into a list of priorities. Those on top are the ones you must see action on soon; those lower down can wait.

At this point you have a couple of choices available to you. If staff members were fairly receptive to your concerns during the initial visit, you may want to meet again with just those individuals. If they were very reserved or even negative in their responses, you may want to request a joint conference with the teachers and the principal. In either case, *call the teacher first* to inform him or her of your plans.

Enter the conference accepting the fact that the teaching staff is comprised of professionals trained and experienced in meeting the educational needs of children. At the same time, take responsibility for your child's education. Explain your top priority concerns and discuss the ways in which you and your child plan to contribute to a solution.

Having met everyone halfway, you now have a good chance of soliciting some possible solutions from them. Ask them to list all of the options available to you by way of changes in curriculum, program, or instructional techniques. For purposes of the discussion, add to their list those you developed in your own preparation.

Once the staff has presented to you the solutions they find acceptable, it is up to you to choose the one you feel is best suited to your child. If necessary, you have every right to insist that there *will be* options.

That is, you have every right to insist that there will be *reasonable* options. Remember that the further a child is from the norm, the more of a challenge he or she presents to the school system. On any given day, each teacher must balance the needs of many different children of widely varying abilities. Sometimes children with special needs may be grouped in some way for similar instruction; at other times, highly gifted children may require an individual plan. As schools are not set up to handle individual plans, this is a major adjustment to ask them to make, and you should be aware of this.

Public elementary schools are primarily academic in nature, so it may not be reasonable to expect a great deal of special programming for the child whose talents lie beyond their scope. A typical first-grade classroom is simply not equipped to provide serious training in music, and for a child with special ability in that area the responsibility will fall back on the family. (For suggestions on where to find various enrichment opportunities, see page 122.)

Running the Roadblocks

There are some common objections to programming for high-ability children that are *not* acceptable, so you need not accept them. Following are some that parents often find themselves facing — and reasons why they are usually invalid.

Roadblock

"High-ability children will do fine on their own. After all, they have so much going for them."

While some gifted children do well in school, a significant number do not. Studies indicate that many typical classrooms actually hold such children back. Not only does this lead to a loss of learning potential, but the resulting stress the child experiences from being bored, as well as the damage done to his or her self-esteem, can be great. Even those gifted children who seem to fit the curriculum often do so at great expense to themselves, either masking their ability or becoming tense "short adults" who invest massive amounts of energy in doing exactly what the teacher requires of them. Social problems are common.

Roadblock

"Educators know what's best for children. As a parent, you are not a teacher and should leave educational decisions to the schools."

Parents know their children very well, especially during the early years. If you have done some reading in the field of gifted education, you are probably as well-versed on the subject as many educators.

As an individual who pays taxes and/or tuition, you are a consumer of educational services. You have as many rights in this area as in any other. You are not required to accept inferior goods from merchants or inappropriate services from doctors, attorneys, or mechanics. In fact, consumer advocates advise you to do the opposite: to insist on a quality product or service that meets your needs. The same holds true for schools — or at least it should.

Roadblock

"The school district has other special-needs children who are more deserving or in need of service."

This is not an either/or situation. Most school districts have in print and available to the public a philosophy statement. Ask to see that statement. Usually it will make reference to taking children at "all levels" or from "all backgrounds" (or some similar phrasing) and moving them forward educationally. Use this as your ammunition and insist that the system comply with its own stated philosophy and take *your* child forward from his or her existing level of need.

Roadblock

"Gifted programming is elitist and makes other children feel bad."

Gifted programming is elitist only if that is the attitude of the staff. A good program promotes a positive attitude about self-worth regardless of ability.

In addition, gifted children should not be asked to sacrifice an appropriate education to the needs of other children. This is analogous to telling a child in a wheelchair, "Your chair clogs the traffic in the hallway and is bothersome to the other students. Please do without it." While special-needs individuals must make some adjustments for the good of all, other adjustments — such as putting up with twelve years of inappropriate schoolwork — are absurd.

Roadblock

"High-ability kids are often divergent thinkers and are known to act out in class. The school will consider a special program when the high-potential kids earn it by proving that they know how to get along with everyone and follow the rules."

That's confusing behavior with educational need. Special-needs children merit appropriate programming because it is the mission of the schools to provide adequately for each child. This is true whether the need stems from a handicap, a difficult home situation, or exceptionally high ability. Would a school deny blind students access to Braille materials until they modified their behavior so their blindness was no longer a nuisance to their instructors or fellow students? Neither should gifted children be required to "earn" an appropriate program.

Roadblock

"It is dangerous to label young children. We might make a mistake at this early age. Besides, it's better to just let them be children for awhile."

Asking for an appropriate program is not asking that gifted children be treated as short adults, nor that they be denied the playful activities of primary classrooms. Instead, it is asking that they not be made to repeat materials they have already mastered, or materials they master very quickly. Given the problems that some gifted children have, many of which take root in the very early years, it is dangerous *not* to have such a program. In addition, if the program is appropriately structured, the children need not be labeled at all.

It is sufficient to say at this point that your child would benefit from an enriched program in math (or language arts, or science). If the situation changes, so will the placement.

Roadblock

"Young children need social skills. If we separate them from other children, they will become social isolates. Many of them have social problems already, and substituting another option for the standard curriculum would only make them worse."

First, not all gifted children have social problems. Second, for those who do it is frequently the result of not having real peers with whom to interact. They need other children of like age *and ability*, not just agemates from whom they feel different.

Again, this is confusing curriculum with social issues. In essence, this policy says to children, "You are having trouble relating to peers. As a strategy for addressing this problem, we will place you in a room full of children from whom you feel different. We will then ask you to spend a great deal of time doing activities that you find repetitive and boring. When you get good and frustrated with this situation and act out toward your classmates and teachers, we will say, 'See, we knew you needed work on social skills.'"

Teaching reading is teaching reading; teaching social behaviors is teaching social behaviors. One should not be confused with the other. It's possible to teach them simultaneously, but this happens when strategies are specifically and carefully designed to have that effect.

☐ ■ ☐

One mother recalls a particularly awful period during her son's first year of school. He had been acting out to a ferocious extent

— regularly interrupting the teacher, demanding attention, distracting the other children, and generally causing chaos in the classroom.

The mother began by trying to work with the system. There were several lengthy conferences, and meanwhile the situation continued to escalate. Her son was sent home and threatened with expulsion. Mom continued to support the teacher's efforts, even when she did not personally agree with some of the ways the teacher was approaching the problem.

"It felt like the teacher and I had joined forces against Jacob," she says. "He would be corrected at school, and I was expected to reinforce that correction at home by making him stay in his room, putting him to bed early, cutting out all special treats. Not only was he miserable at school; he was miserable at home. And so was I.

"Finally it hit me: If I wouldn't stand up for him, who would? Who else would be my child's champion? From that day forward, we began to make progress. The teacher started to learn about giftedness and ways to meet the needs of gifted children. It was slow — it's still slow — but now there's hope."

As you continue to advocate for your child in the present, consider the long haul. Our children are going to be in some school system for a minimum of 12 years. Crisis intervention may be necessary, but it isn't enough. Perhaps it's time for you to join or form an advocacy group of other parents who will lobby for appropriate educational opportunities. We offer the final pages of this book as a place to start.

"Our Hero!"

PART IV

RESOURCES

Directory of Organizations

State Parent Associations

Associations for parents of gifted children have been established in most states and the District of Columbia. You can reap as many or as few benefits from joining as you choose. Depending on the organization, they hold meetings and conventions, produce newsletters and other special publications, and bring in guest speakers. Most importantly, they provide a support network for parents of children with special abilities and special needs. If there isn't one close to you, write another to find out the best way to start one in your area.*

ALASKA
Alaskans for Gifted and Talented
Education
Marcia Romick
PO Box 1250
Fairbanks, AK 99701

ARIZONA
Arizona Association for Gifted
and Talented
Nina Arias Nelson
1025 East Port Au Prince
Phoenix, AZ 85022

ARKANSAS
Arkansans for Gifted and
Talented Education
Rick Tremblay
1 Spike Cove
Pine Bluff, AR 71602

CALIFORNIA
California Association
for the Gifted
Sharon Mountford
23684 Shoenborn Street
Canoga Park, CA 91304

COLORADO
Colorado Association for Gifted
and Talented
Kaye Wergedal
PO Box 10845 UP Station
Denver, CO 80210

CONNECTICUT
Connecticut Association
for Gifted
Sherry Earle
10 First Street
Danbury, CT 06810

---

* To the best of our knowledge, the information in this section is accurate as of May, 1986. However, many state parent associations elect new officers annually. If the person you write to no longer heads his or her respective organization, your letter will likely be forwarded.

DELAWARE
Delaware Talented and Gifted
Melody Young
204 Gordy Place
New Castle, DE 19720

DISTRICT OF COLUMBIA
District of Columbia PAG TAG
Toni Ford
3150 Cherry Road N.E.
Washington, DC 20018

FLORIDA
Florida Association for the Gifted
Donna Kellam, President
13832 Hunterwood Road
Jacksonville, FL 32225

GEORGIA
Georgia Supporters for Gifted
and Talented
Ruth S. Cowan
4065 Maxey Hill Drive
Stone Mountain, GA 30083

HAWAII
Hawaii Association for
Intellectually Gifted Children
PO Box 22878
Honolulu, HI 96822

ILLINOIS
Illinois Council for Gifted and
Talented
Trevor Steinbach
556 Carlyle Lane
Bolingbrook, IL 60439

INDIANA
Indiana Association for Gifted
and Talented
Ken Walker
200 Marigold
Terre Haute, IN 47803

Central Indiana Association
for Gifted Children
Jill Meisenheimer, President
3923 Kitty Hawk Court
Carmel, IN 46032

IOWA
Mississippi Bend Area
Education Agency
ITAG
Jan Yoder, President
729 21st Street
Bettendorf, IA 52722

KANSAS
Kansas Association for Gifted/
Talented/Creative
Debbie Haltom
1909 North Calhoun
Liberal, KS 67901

KENTUCKY
Kentucky Association
for Gifted Education
Julia Roberts
College of Education
311 Western Kentucky University
Bowling Green, KY 42101

LOUISIANA
Gifted/Talented Consultant
Jefferson Parish Public
School System
501 Manhattan Boulevard
Harvey, LA 70058

Association for Gifted and
Talented Students
Kay Coffee
1627 Frankfort
New Orleans, LA 70122

MARYLAND
Maryland Coalition for Gifted
and Talented
Jingle Lutz
726 Tiffany Court
Gaithersburg, MD 20878

Maryland Council for Gifted
and Talented
Betty Stauffer
14404 Chesterfield Road
Rockville, MD 20853

MASSACHUSETTS

Massachusetts Association for
Advancement of Individual
Potential
Diana Reeves
Box 65
Milton Village, MA 02187

MICHIGAN

Michigan Alliance
for Gifted Education
Barb Davis
Eaton ISD
1790 E. Packard Hwy.
Charlotte, MI 48813

Michigan Association
for the Academically Talented
Katy Lux
927 Iroquois SE
Grand Rapids, MI 49506

MINNESOTA

Minnesota Council for Gifted
and Talented
5701 Normandale Road
Minneapolis, MN 55424

MISSISSIPPI

Mississippi Association
for Talented and Gifted
Melissa Grantham
836 Arlington St.
Jackson, MS 39202

MONTANA

Montana Association for Gifted
and Talented
Paula Fascilla
473 3rd Avenue NE
Kalispell, MT 59901

MISSOURI

Gifted Association of Missouri
Sue Cole, President
844 Rodney Vista Boulevard
Cape Girardeau, MO 63701

NEBRASKA

Nebraska Association for Gifted
and Talented
Dennis F. Flood
Elkhorn Public Schools
502 Glenn Street
Elkhorn, NE 68022

NEVADA

Nevada Association for Gifted
and Talented
Duane L. Lawrence
1207 Arrowhead
Las Vegas, NV 89106

Academically Talented Parents
Council
Mary Musson
5254 San Anselmo Street
Las Vegas, NV 89120

NEW HAMPSHIRE

New Hampshire Support
Association for Gifted Education
Mary White
PO Box 566
Hampstead, NH 03841

NEW JERSEY

New Jersey Gifted Child
Society Inc.
Gina Ginsberg Riggs
190 Rock Road
Glen Rock, NJ 07452

NEW MEXICO

Albuquerque Association for
Gifted and Talented Students
Judy Hudenko
13208 Casa Bonita Drive NE
Albuquerque, NM 87111

NEW YORK

Advocacy for Gifted Education in
the State of New York (AGATE)
Virginia Z. Ehrlich
23 Wilder Road
Suffern, NY 10901

NORTH CAROLINA
Parents for the Advancement of
Gifted Education
of North Carolina
Don Russell
900 Brintonial Way
Winston Salem, NC 27104

OHIO
Ohio Association
for Gifted Children
Nina Crosby
7927 Hickory Hill Lane
Cincinnati, OH 45241

OKLAHOMA
Oklahoma Association for the
Gifted/Creative/Talented Inc.
PO Box 53276
Capitol Complex
Oklahoma City, OK 73152

OREGON
Oregon Association for Talented
and Gifted
PO Box 1703
Beaverton, OR 97075

PENNSYLVANIA
Pennsylvania Association for
Gifted Education (PAGE)
Irena Sandler
PO Box 8
New Britain, PA 18901

RHODE ISLAND
State Advocates
of Gifted Education
SAGE of Rhode Island
Barbara Reis
42 Oregon Avenue
North Providence, RI 02911

SOUTH DAKOTA
South Dakota Talented
and Gifted
Carolyn Nelson
2545 Harriet Lane
Sioux Falls, SD 57103

TENNESSEE
Tennessee Association for Gifted
and Talented
621 Hunter's Lane
Brentwood, TN 37027

Tennessee Association
for the Gifted (TAG)
Judy Collins
Route 12, Box 45
Lebanon, TN 37087

TEXAS
Texas Association for the Gifted
and Talented
PO Box 1991
Austin, TX 78767

UTAH
Utah Parents Association for
Gifted/Talented
GiGi Brandt
2059 E. Ninth South
Salt Lake City, UT 84108

VERMONT
Vermont Council
for the Education of the Gifted,
Creative and Talented
Janet McKinnon
116 South Main Street
Middlebury, VT 05753

VIRGINIA
Virginia Association for
the Education of the Gifted
Marlene Blum
2417 Luckett Avenue
Vienna, VA 22180

WASHINGTON
Northwest Gifted Child
Association
Dan McDonald Ph.D.
PO Box 1226
Bellevue, WA 98009

Washington Association
of Education for Talented
and Gifted
Altamai Whitehill
520 4th Street
Cheney, WA 99014

WEST VIRGINIA
West Virginia Gifted Education
Association
Linda Jones
131 E. 6th Street
Williamstown, WV 26187

WISCONSIN
Wisconsin Council for the Gifted
and Talented
Beecham Robinson
3621 West Allerton Avenue
Greenfield, WI 53221

WYOMING
Wyoming Association for Gifted
Education
Jory Westberry
426 M Street
Rock Springs, WY 82901

State Education Organizations

In many states the office of education has a department or an individual charged with the responsibility for gifted and talented school-age children. The level of service may range from the minimum of answering basic questions to greater levels of involvement, such as monitoring school programs or mandating special services.

Contact these departments with questions regarding state and local funding, legislative action, and the nature of state and local programs. They may also be able to put you in touch with other resources in your area.

ALABAMA
Specialist for Gifted and Talented
Program for Exceptional
Children and Youth
Alabama State Department
of Education
1020 Monticello Court
Montgomery,AL 36117

ALASKA
Programs for Gifted and Talented
Section for Exceptional Children
Pouch F
Alaska Office Building
Juneau, AK 99811

ARIZONA
Gifted and Talented Specialist
Arizona Department
of Education
1535 West Jefferson
Phoenix, AZ 85007

ARKANSAS
Office of Gifted and Talented
Education
Room 105C Education Building
4 Capitol Mall
Little Rock, AR 72201

CALIFORNIA
Programs for Gifted and Talented
721 Capitol Mall
Sacramento, CA 95814

COLORADO
Gifted and Talented Student
Programming
Colorado Department
of Education
201 East Colfax
Denver, CO 80203

CONNECTICUT
The Connecticut Association
for the Gifted
PO Box 2219
Hartford, CT 06145

DELAWARE
State Supervisor, Gifted and
Talented Programs
Delaware Department
of Public Instruction
PO Box 1402
Dover, DE 19903

DISTRICT OF COLUMBIA
Gifted and Talented Education
Program
Bryan School
13th Street and Independence
Ave. SE
Washington, DC 20003

FLORIDA
Florida Association for the Gifted
1520 Sprinkle Drive
Jacksonville, FL 32211

GEORGIA
Coordinator
Program for the Gifted
Georgia Department of Education
Twin Towers East, Suite 1970
Atlanta, GA 30334

HAWAII
Gifted/Talented
Department of Education
189 Lunalilo Home Road
Honolulu, HI 96825

IDAHO
Gifted and Talented Programs
Len B. Jordan Building
Boise, ID 83720

ILLINOIS
Gifted and Talented Programs
Illinois State Board of Education
100 North First Street
Springfield, IL 62777

INDIANA
Office of Gifted Talented
Education
Ball State University
Shared Information Services
Burris Lab School
2001 University Avenue
Muncie, IN 47306

IOWA
Gifted and Talented Programs
Department of Public Instruction
Grimes State Office Building
Des Moines, IA 50319

KANSAS
Kansas Department of Education
120 East 10th Street
Topeka, KS 66612

KENTUCKY
Gifted and Talented Programs
Bureau of Instruction
1830 Capital Plaza Tower
Frankfort, KY 40601

LOUISIANA
Gifted and Talented Programs
Department of Education
PO Box 94064, Capitol Station
Baton Rouge, LA 70804-9064

MAINE
Gifted and Talented Programs
Special Education Division
State House Station 23
Augusta, ME 04333

MICHIGAN
Specialist, Gifted and Talented
Programs
Michigan Department
of Education
PO Box 30008
Lansing, MI 48909

MINNESOTA
Gifted and Talented Programs
641 Capital Square
St. Paul, MN 55101

MISSISSIPPI
Gifted and Talented Programs
Division of Special Education
PO Box 771
Jackson, MS 39205

MISSOURI
Center for Gifted Education
Drury College
900 North Benton
Springfield, MO 65804

MONTANA
Gifted and Talented Programs
Office of Public Instruction
State Capitol
Helena, MT 59620

NEBRASKA
Gifted and Talented Programs
Division of Special Education
301 Centennial Mall South
Lincoln, NE 68509

NEVADA
Gifted and Talented Programs
Department of Education
Division of Special Education
400 West King Street
Carson City, NV 89710

NEW HAMPSHIRE
Gifted Education
New Hampshire
State Department of Education
101 Pleasant Street
Concord, NH 03301

NEW JERSEY
Gifted and Talented Programs
Academic Education Division
225 West State Street CN-500
Trenton, NJ 08625
Attention: Jeanne Carlson

NEW MEXICO
Gifted and Talented Programs
Division of Special Education
Room 125
Santa Fe, NM 87503

NEW YORK
Gifted and Talented Programs
Department of Education
320 A Main Building
Albany, NY 12234

NORTH CAROLINA
Academically Gifted Programs
Department of Public Instruction
116 West Edenton Street
Raleigh, NC 27603-1712

NORTH DAKOTA
Gifted and Talented Programs
State Capitol
Bismarck, ND 58505

OHIO

Gifted and Talented Programs
Division of Special Education
933 High Street
Worthington, OH 43085

OKLAHOMA

Gifted and Talented Programs
Department of Education
2500 North Lincoln Blvd.
Oliver Hodge Memorial Bldg.
Suite 315
Oklahoma City, OK 73105

OREGON

TAG Program
(Talented and Gifted)
Eugene School District
200 North Monroe Street
Eugene, OR 97402

PENNSYLVANIA

Gifted and Talented Programs
Bureau of Special Education
333 Market Street
Harrisburg, PA 17126

RHODE ISLAND

Gifted and Talented Programs
Department of Educatino
Roger Williams Building
22 Hayes Street
Providence, RI 02908

SOUTH CAROLINA

Gifted and Talented Programs
Rutledge Building Room 803
1429 Senate Street
Columbia, SC 29201

SOUTH DAKOTA

Gifted and Talented Programs
Division of Education
700 N. Illinois
Pierre, SD 57501

TENNESSEE

Gifted and Talented Programs
Department of Education
132 Cordell Hull Building
Nashville, TN 37219

TEXAS

Division of Gifted/Talented
Education
Texas Education Agency
William B. Travis Building
1701 North Congress
Austin, TX 78701

UTAH

State Director
Utah State Office of Education
250 East 500 South
Salt Lake City, UT 84111

VERMONT

Gifted Consultant
Vermont Department
of Education
Montpelier, VT 05602

VIRGINIA

Programs for the Gifted
State Department of Education
PO Box 6Q
Richmond, VA 23216

WASHINGTON

Gifted and Talented Programs
Supervisor
Division of Special Service and
Professional Programs
Old Capitol Building FG-11
Olympia, WA 98504

WEST VIRGINIA

Gifted and Talented Programs
Division of Special Education
Capitol Complex Building #6
Room B-304
Charleston, WV 25305

WISCONSIN
Gifted and Talented Programs
Department of Public Instruction
126 Langdon Street
Madison, WI 53702

WYOMING
Gifted and Talented Programs
Hathaway Building
Cheyenne, WY 82002

UNITED STATES POSSESSIONS

AMERICAN SAMOA
Programs for Gifted and Talented
Department of Special Education
Pago Pago, American Samoa

GUAM
Gifted and Talented Education
Program
Division of Special Education
PO Box DE
Agana, Guam 96910

MARSHALL ISLANDS
Gifted and Talented Programs
EBEYE TAG
E.C.E.S.
EBEYE, Marshall Islands, 96970

PUERTO RICO
Gifted and Talented Programs
Office of External Services
Department of Education
Hato Rey, PR 00924

SAIPAN
Coordinator
Federal Programs/Gifted
Talented Ed.
Division of Education TTPI
PO Box 27 CHRB
Capital Hill, Saipan 96950

VIRGIN ISLANDS
State Office of Special Education
PO Box 6640
St. Thomas, VI 00801

CANADA

ONTARIO
Ontario Association for Bright Children
2 Bloor St. West
Suite 100 – 156
Toronto, Ontario
M4W 2G7

National Organizations for the Gifted

National organizations for gifted children provide a variety of services to parents and educators. Often their journals contain more detailed and research-oriented material than those published by the state organizations. Their conventions feature state-of-the-art presentations in areas such as the development of intelligence, educational programming, and creativity theory. Primarily geared toward theorists and professionals, national organizations can still be of value to a highly interested parent.

American Association for Gifted
Children
15 Gramercy Park
New York, NY 10003

Association for the Gifted
Council for Exceptional Children
1920 Association Drive
Reston, VA 22091

ERIC Clearinghouse on
Handicapped and Gifted
Children
1920 Association Drive
Reston, VA 22091

Gifted Child Society Inc.
190 Rock Road
Glen Rock, NJ 07452

Creative Education Foundation
437 Franklin Street
Buffalo, NY 14202

National Association for Child
Care Management
1255 23rd Street NW
Washington, DC 20037

National Association for Creative
Children and Adults
8080 Springvalley Drive
Cincinnati, OH 45236

National Association
for Gifted Children
Lovell Professional Building
4175 Lovell Road Suite 140
Circle Pines, MN 55014

National State Leadership
Training Institute on the Gifted
and Talented
316 West 2nd Street Suite PH-C
Los Angeles, CA 90012-3595

World Council for Gifted and
Talented Children
Box 218
Teacher's College
Columbia University
525 W. 120th Street
New York, NY 10027

For Further Reading

Books of Interest to Parents of Gifted Children

Very little material is available that is specific to the needs of parents of young gifted children. Instead, parents wishing at this time to read more about giftedness will have to cull from books on related topics. Listed below are several that parents in similar circumstances have found helpful. Some are childrearing books with emphasis on issues relevant to parents of high-ability children; some are general books on parenting the gifted which make at least some reference to the needs of young children; some are intended for professionals, but parents may want to peruse them as well.

Push/Don't Push

A heated debate is being waged among early childhood specialists regarding the relative merits and dangers of exposing young children to very enriched learning environments. On one side are those who claim that intense early stimulation will permanently improve a child's ability to think; on the other are those who suggest that such early "interference"with a child's natural timetable will have lasting negative effects on his or her emotional health and psychological well-being.

Listed below are books from both sides of the argument. Those warning of the dangers of pushing children offer effective arguments and strategies for parents who wish to avoid the pitfall of appearing to value a gifted child's accomplishments more than the child himself or herself. With these cautions firmly in mind, you may want to peruse the "push" books for home learning activities.

Ames, L.B. and J.A. Chase, *Don't Push Your Preschooler* (New York: Harper & Row, 1974).

"It speaks well for American optimism that so many have so much confidence in their ability to push children along....It speaks less well for our good sense or our judgment, or our ability to learn from past experience" (page 4). Within this philosophy are presented various theories of development, most of which are explained in greater detail in other works listed here. The main value of this book is the clear distinction made between meeting the legitimate needs of the truly gifted learner and placing unnecessary pressure on a child because one hopes to "make" the child gifted. Despite the negative admonition of the title, the book gives many positive suggestions, all of them based on the need to relax and enjoy.

Beck, J., *How To Raise a Brighter Child: The Case for Early Learning* (New York: Pocket Books, 1975).

"Simple, effective ways to increase your child's I.Q. by 20 points or more" — that's what the cover of this book promises. The background information is there, the evidence indicates that the activities really will improve I.Q. scores, but the tone is stridently pushy. Persons who question the validity of this teach-to-the-test philosophy are airily dismissed as closed-minded or outdated. The book is full of good ideas that would be helpful to parents wishing to stimulate a bright youngster, but it should only be read with part of the mind firmly fixed on the difference between encouragement and pressure.

Elkind, David, *The Hurried Child: Growing Up Too Fast Too Soon* (Reading, Massachusetts: Addison-Wesley Publishing Co., 1981).

Elkind, a child psychologist, discusses the dynamics of hurrying children in such areas as the home, the school, and the media. His challenges to those he feels are stressing children are specific and pointed. While this book is written about all ages, it does refer to young children, and the problems the author describes in older children clearly begin at an early age.

Engelmann, Siegried and Therese, *Give Your Child a Superior Mind* (New York: Simon and Schuster, 1981).

As its title implies, this book falls squarely into the early stimulation camp. For parents who believe that theory, it contains many suggestions for initiating learning experiences with a child. Parents who prefer to wait until their child indicates an interest in a particular skill can ignore the strongly worded admonitions to "teach now" and instead stockpile some of the ideas for when they seem useful and appropriate.

Hainstock, Elizabeth, *Teaching Montessori in the Home* (New York: New American Library, 1968).

Very specific instructional strategies for parents to use at home. Based on the Montessori method, all activities fall into the lifeskills category or more academic categories.

Johnson, Robert Leland, *Super Babies* (Smithtown, New York: Exposition Press, 1982).

This will be of interest to parents who are wondering about "those babies from out East who are learning Japanese and can recognize Picassos." It is the story of one child whose parents follow the program of the Institute for the Achievement of Human Potential. It is anecdotal in nature and strident in tone, a strong proponent of the "earlier and more is better" philosophy.

LeShan, Eda, *The Conspiracy Against Childhood* (New York: Atheneum Publishers, 1980).

The first portion of this book offers some of the most strongly presented arguments against pushing young children that can be found anywhere. As the book progresses, the focus moves to older children, with variations on the same theme. Some of the concerns raised about overly sophisticated coursework seem to ignore the fact that not all children are forced to move at this advanced pace, but actually choose it. Still, many of the points are well taken. A chapter heading, "Any Dope Can Have a High I.Q.," may at first seem offensive, but the issues raised in it about the overemphasis on testing are valid. You may or may not agree with this book, but it will make you think about issues important to your child.

Ludington-Hoe, Susan, *How To Have a Smarter Baby* (New York: Rawson Associates, 1985).
    Starts with prenatal nutrition, works its way through stimulation *in utero*, and offers strategies for infant stimulation. The activities are definitely designed and billed to accelerate development, and the evidence is that they will. Again, many good ideas are offered, but a wise parent will balance their benefits with those of a more relaxed parenting style.

Giftedness

Listed below are some books written for parents of gifted children. They are recommended over other similar works for one of two reasons: Either they contain at least some reference to young children, or the focus is such that the information presented can be adapted to the needs of younger children. Remember, though, that a five-year-old child, regardless of how bright or talented, is a very different animal from a nine-year-old of similar ability. Research on young gifted children is not nearly as advanced as that on older children, and it is inappropriate to assume that what applies at one age applies equally at another.

Alvino, James and the Editors of Gifted Children Monthly, *Parents' Guide to Raising a Gifted Child: Recognizing and Developing Your Child's Potential* (New York: Little, Brown and Co., 1985).
    An exceptionally comprehensive parenting book that does sometimes address the needs of younger children. Its intended audience is definitely parents, and it sticks to points of interest to them. Recommended for your home reference library.

Dixon, John Philo, *The Spatial Child* (Springfield, Illinois: Charles C. Thomas, 1983).
    A far more technical book than others recommended here. Included for parents with markedly spatial children — kids who can build whole LEGOS villages at age three but may or may not be able to read fluently even by school age. Dixon builds a case that these children experience their own kind of discrimination in a school setting and offers some strategies

for coping. Of interest if you have a child like this and are concerned.

Hall, Eleanor and Nancy Skinner, *Somewhere to Turn: Strategies for Parents of the Gifted and Talented* (New York: Teachers College Press, 1980).
Gives specific advice on identification, parent enrichment strategies, and resources outside the home. The first section is devoted to preschool issues.

Lehane, S., *The Creative Child* (Englewood Cliffs, New Jersey: Prentice-Hall, 1979).
Specific suggestions for promoting and/or dealing with creative behavior in preschool and early elementary school aged children. Objectives (for example, "coping with emotions through fantasy") are accompanied by an idea or two for parents to try.

Lowenfeld, V., *Your Child and His Art* (New York: Macmillan Co., 1957).
Very specific responses to parents' questions concerning the artistic development of their children. Deals mainly with average children, but some special attention is given to the gifted in a separate chapter. All parents will find the descriptions of various stages of artistic development helpful. Emphasis is placed on art as a *spontaneous* and very personal reaction to life experience.

Meekstroth, Elizabeth, Stephanie Tolan, and James Webb, *Guiding the Gifted Child* (Columbus, Ohio: Ohio Psychology Publishing Co., 1982).
Focuses on emotional and social issues. Each chapter gives information on a topic and then answers frequently-asked questions. Will be most helpful as children reach ages seven and up.

Perino, Sheila C. and Joseph, *Parenting the Gifted: Developing the Promise* (New York: R.R. Bowker Co., 1981).
The authors are self-proclaimed "parent and child advocates." This book covers the gifted child from infancy to adolescence. It helps you learn the language, including definitions and/or how the term *gifted* is "really" used. It includes

some interesting developmental charts based on the Denver Development standards, listing typical ages at which certain behaviors might be expected and comparing these by percentage to children who develop earlier. This would be a particularly helpful work for the parent who suspects his or her child to be of above-average ability but needs some encouragement and confidence-building.

Vail, Priscilla, *The World of the Gifted Child* (New York: Walker and Company, 1979).

This book has a readable, humorous style full of anecdotes. Vail is an educator but writes from a personal perspective. Of particular interest are her feelings regarding grade-skipping, because they would apply equally to issues of early school entrance.

Good Reading Anytime

The following book is not part of the push/don't push debate, nor does it deal specifically with giftedness. Instead, it's a general child-development work — one that consistently gets positive reviews from parents of bright children.

Fraiberg, S.H. *The Magic Years* (New York: Scribner's Sons, 1959).

An absolutely delightful examination of the early years of childhood, focusing on emotional development. From her vast experience as a clinical child psychologist, Dr. Fraiberg synthesizes a number of theories of child development into one witty, commonsensical yet challenging description of a child's growth to maturity. Although she never directly addresses questions of ability, many of the case studies cited seem to be of high-ability children caught in the classic conflict between age-level emotions and above-level intellect. If you've only got time to read one book, make it this one.

Publications on the Theme of Giftedness

Magazines and journals are a good way to keep up with current developments in the field of gifted education. They offer information on the latest theories and research regarding intelligence, talent, and creativity.

Primarily for Parents

G/C/T Magazine
Box 6448
Mobile, AL 36660
Annual subscription price:
$24 (6 issues)

Gifted Children Monthly
PO Box 115
Sewell, NY 08080
Annual subscription price:
$24 (11 issues)

For Parents and Educators

The Roeper Review, A Journal on Gifted Education
PO Box 329
Bloomfield Hills, MI 48013
Subscription rates (4 issues/year):
    Individual: 2 years $40,
    1 year $22
    Institution: 2 years $45,
    1 year $30

Esoteric but Interesting

Exceptional Children
1920 Association Drive
Reston, VA 22091
Annual subscription price
(CEC dues): $30 (6 issues)

Gifted Child Quarterly
4175 Lovell Road Suite 140
Circle Pines, MN 55014
Annual subscription price
(NAGC dues): $20 (4 issues)

Journal of Creative Behavior
Creative Education Foundation
437 Franklin Street
Buffalo, NY 14202
Annual subscription prices
(4 issues):
United States residents: $14
Canada and Mexico: $18
Elsewhere: $24

Index